Celebrating
WOODLAND POND

10th ANNIVERSARY EDITION

RICHARD V. BARRY

Winterlight Books

Shelbyville, KY USA

www.winterlightbooks.net

Celebrating Woodland Pond
by Richard V. Barry

First Printing – July 2019
ISBN: 978-1-68111-312-8

Printed in the U.S.A.

0   1   2   3   4   5   6

BOOKS BY RICHARD V. BARRY

Short Stories

CROSSCURRENTS: Stories of People in Conflict

PERSONAL WARS

INFINITE GESTURES

Novels

AN INCONVENIENT DEATH

QUALITIES OF MERCY

IN EVIL'S VORTEX

MURDER AND CONDO-MONIUM

Novella

HISTORY OF THE SMILING YOUNG LORD

Non-Fiction

EXPERIENCING WOODLAND POND

MISADVENTURES IN EUROPE

DAYS OF DELIGHT AND DESPAIR

DEDICATION

TO Michelle Gramoglia whose outstanding leadership skills, empathic nature and personal commitment to Woodland Pond create the atmosphere in which we all thrive;

TO our dedicated and caring staff who every day enhance our lives;

TO the "Saints" and the "Sinners," and you know who you are;

ONCE AGAIN, TO all the citizens of this much-loved community, bonded in caring for one another.

SPECIAL THANKS to Ann Hanover for applying her meticulous proofreading skills to this book in manuscript form.

"Seize now and here the hour that is, nor trust some later day."

–Horace

"Who well lives, long lives; for this age of ours should not be numbered by years, days and hours."

–Cervantes

"From quiet homes and first beginning
   Out to the undiscovered ends,
There's nothing worth the wear of winning
   But laughter and the love of friends."

–Hilaire Belloc

"What do we live for, if it is not to make life less difficult for each other?"

–George Eliot's *Middlemarch*

Table of Contents

Bringing Things Up To Date

Six years ago, after living at Woodland Pond for two years, I interrupted my writing in various fictional genres to record my very happy experiences since joining the Woodland Pond community. I began that book with an assertive declaration, "This is a love story!"

Now, six years later, in conjunction with the tenth anniversary of Woodland Pond's opening, I again return to recording my unfolding life, and I think it fitting that I should begin this book with a similar declaration: The Love Story Continues! Indeed, my personal happiness, contentment and productivity have only increased as, simultaneously, I have seen great changes and improvements contributing to Woodland Pond's welfare and growth.

When I acknowledge how I am surrounded by so many vital, interesting residents, equally dedicated to nourishing the physical, mental, emotional and spiritual planes of their lives, and how all our efforts along these lines are eagerly encouraged and actively supported by our very caring, superbly trained staff, I feel amply justified in the private name I have given to my community: The Happy Home.

One has only to read our monthly newsletter and the accompanying monthly calendar of events to appreciate the full scope of daily activities, residents' committee meetings, special interest groups, support services, cultural excursions as well as cultural events on campus, luncheon adventures, administrative presentations and opportunities for residents to interact with the wider world through volunteer service, all of which offer rich, variegated stimulation for us "Ponders."

I have frequently said that I feel as though I am on a first-class cruise ship that never leaves port, and each day provides me ample choices on how best to spend my time, combining, if I choose, entertainment and the pleasure of lively company with my fellow residents as well as physical exercise and mental enrichment.

In looking back over my soon-to-be eight years of residency at Woodland Pond, I am most grateful that I made the decision to join this community when I was still a reasonably young seventy-four, enjoying good health and an active lifestyle, for this condition allowed me to take full advantage of all that the community had to offer. I continued to spend most of the winter in Puerto Rico, continued to travel widely, and continued with outside interests. Whenever I travelled, I had merely to stop my mail and lock my door, with no other cares to concern me. While at home I could also engage in the many daily activities enumerated above.

Woodland Pond is a community where residents play a very active role in monitoring and advising the management on all aspects of daily life, putting to good use the professional skills they have honed over the many years of their working lives. The impressive total number of resident committees attests to residents' dynamic participation. I, too, enjoyed contributing to my beloved community through committee service.

Over the course of several years I served on various committees. I was a member of the Health Committee and had the singular pleasure of working with Michelle Gramoglia, our outstanding young President and CEO, on creating a Transition Guide to Assisted Living. Another rewarding experience was serving for three years as the chair of the Nominating Committee, recruiting residents to serve on our vitally active Residents' Council. Serving on the Décor and Design Committee and the Dining Committee also proved to be worthwhile, rewarding endeavors. For three years I further enjoyed leading the group discussions of One Book, One New Paltz, when the discussions were scheduled at Woodland Pond for both Woodland Pond and New Paltz residents.

For several years I was a member of the Pondaliers, a group of resident singers, guided by a licensed choral instructor. The group gives two recitals each year, always well attended and enthusiastically received by the community. I also participated in the Playreaders, where residents read plays under the tutelage of a retired SUNY New Paltz professor. I wrote several short satirical plays for this group that were performed for our fellow residents. (They love to laugh!)

With two swim buddies, Dr. Paul Lurie, who passed away in April, 2019 at the age of 101, and Marilyn Dilascio, a former long-distance open-water swimmer honored in the Canadian Sports Hall of Fame, I swam laps each morning at 6 am in our heated indoor pool. After my retirement from the field of educational administration and as a teacher of teachers, I became a full-time writer. I discovered that I could arrange my life at Woodland Pond to readily accompany this pursuit while also enjoying all the benefits of community living.

Each weekday, as I continued a writing regimen at my desk in my apartment, I only had to glance out of any one of my windows to behold the impressive Shawangunk Mountains at close range as well as the Catskill Mountains off in the distance, fronted by vast acres of preserved land—scenery guaranteed to inspire any writer. My productivity level soared and among my twelve published books, six of them have been written at Woodland Pond.

When my daily, disciplined hours of writing were over, I had many options. In warmer weather I enjoyed the short hike down to Beaver Pond on our property, and yes, most of the time there was a family of beavers busily building their lodge but they were not often visible during the day. On bad-weather days I could go to our gym for a treadmill workout or, if I was feeling lazy, I could go to our library and browse among the thousands of books, all donated by residents from our own private collections. Lunch in the Bistro with open seating was always an occasion for visiting with friends or making new ones, and the Happy Hour in the Pub was forever a time for high spirits, ebullient exchanges and much good cheer.

I especially looked forward to dinner in the Dining Room where I usually had arranged to meet with different sets of friends who always made me laugh and feel thoroughly relaxed. Sharing the latest news, including a modicum of gossip, added zest to our gatherings.

My enjoyment of theater, classical music and opera continued unabated. I could catch a bus into the city, have a nice lunch and attend a matinee performance of a Broadway play. Or I could go to Lincoln Center and see some of the world's greatest ballet companies and orchestras. The Bardavon Theater in Poughkeepsie, only twenty-five minutes away from Woodland Pond, afforded me simultaneous telecasts of operas from the Metropolitan Opera House, and at the same venue I had a season subscription each year to the Hudson Valley Philharmonic.

With so many colleges surrounding us, including SUNY New Paltz, a ten-minute ride away from our door, each month residents can choose five or six events offered at these different venues—lectures, plays, dance recitals, chamber music ensembles, piano competition winners and more—and management provides transportation. Closer to home, on many evenings all I have to do after finishing my dinner is stroll down to our Performing Arts Center (PAC) where I can enjoy similar offerings, including children's recitals under the direction of local dance and piano instructors. On the weekends two current movies, recently released on DVD, are offered in the PAC at both matinee and evening showings.

Our Political Affairs Committee sponsors presentations and question-and-answer forums for residents here at home with political candidates running for various local and county offices. Attendance at these events is always large, signifying the continued interest that residents take in the world beyond our home. For several years I have personally arranged for a New York State Assistant Attorney General to come to Woodland Pond and speak to residents about the latest scams, particularly those that are primarily aimed at senior citizens. Here, too, residents are keen to learn how best to deal with such skullduggery.

The old saying that time flies when you're having fun seems to truly apply in my case, for the years have passed very quickly and it doesn't seem possible that come this September (2019), I'll be celebrating my eighth anniversary of joining Woodland Pond while the community will be celebrating the tenth anniversary of its opening. I still feel singularly blessed to have discovered and moved to Woodland Pond when I did, still young enough to enjoy all its offerings, participate in its many, varied activities and continue an active life of travel, social engagements and cultural pursuits beyond its borders.

I am truly bewildered when I meet people who are considering Woodland Pond as their home but who say they're not ready yet. Honestly, I don't know what that implies. Does it mean that they are not ready to relinquish the multifaceted burdens of home ownership and enjoy a life of ease? Does it mean that they don't prefer to have a life style in which they can devote all their energies to remaining healthy, exploring new horizons and enjoying stimulating friends in a safe, secure and caring environment? In moving to Woodland Pond my life became richer, fuller and more carefree, and I would wish that same pleasurable experience for all prospective residents.

I remember well how a couple, long-time friends of mine but nearly a decade younger, eagerly approved of my coming to Woodland Pond. Then, as the years passed and they were approaching the age at which I had made my big decision, they indicated no interest in making a similar move, preferring to remain in their large, aging house, with all its attendant repairs and upkeep challenges. Whenever I questioned them on their increasingly burdensome home ownership, they uttered vaguely sentimental excuses such as this was where all the memories of their family were connected and they couldn't bear to be parted with so many different collections of things they had accumulated over the years. Suddenly the wife developed permanent health issues that confined her to the main floor of their three-story home, and they had to devise a makeshift bedroom out of their dining room.

When they finally decided that their home was too much of a struggle, they reluctantly sold it. But rather than move to a community like Woodland Pond, they opted to move to a newly built one-story house where they hoped to continue living independently. When I cautiously questioned them on the practicality of such a move, since they were now in their seventies, they expressed a bias—really a fear—against being seen or treated as old in any community comprised of age-restricted residents. "We're just not ready yet," was their emphatic but vague response, and no recounting of the very active lifestyle and the vital, exuberant residents surrounding me seemed to alter their misguided view of life in a community such as mine.

Fate soon delivered another blow when, soon after their move, the husband suffered a heart attack and could no longer attend to his wife's needs without hiring health care workers to assist him with her care. The physical condition of both husband and wife continued to deteriorate until, with much urging from their children, they finally did decide to apply to another CCRC that was closer to their children. By this time they could not qualify for Life Care. They are not rich people and are now spending a good portion of their savings on aides to help them remain in the Independent Living section of their community. If the time comes when they are forced to move into one of the three units in their community's Health Center, their monthly bills will be much higher than if they had come earlier to the community and qualified for Life Care.

When I compare the last very happy and productive eight years of my life to those of this couple's experiences, I find it truly sad that they could not have seen what they considered to be the right move for me as also being the right move for them. Mired in memories, encumbered with a lifetime of accumulated possessions and refusing to acknowledge their age as a time for continued growth and relaxed pleasures in the properly supportive environment, they missed out, I feel, on golden opportunities.

To linger in a home because of memories never made much sense to me since we can carry all our memories with us, wherever we go. To stay in a house because of our accumulated "stuff" also didn't make much sense because the reality is that, sooner or later, we all have to divest ourselves of our "stuff," and I'd rather be the one to decide on what "stuff" I want to keep. In so many cases, children don't even want the "stuff" that their parents treasure. The freedom from excessive cares about too much "stuff" was my reward for making these decisions.

It may be true that some of our residents rely on canes or walkers to assist their mobility, but that should never be misinterpreted as a lack of mental keenness or eager participation in community affairs. Each day our vibrant community pulsates with action as residents happily pursue the many opportunities for physical, mental and social stimulation, afforded by our caring and supportive staff but frequently self-generated by residents, too.

I'm very proud of our community's growth and currently flourishing state, thanks to our remarkable

President and CEO and her extraordinary leadership team, and the vital role residents continue to play in fostering its welfare. Woodland Pond has changed in ways both big and small which, in my view, enhance our daily lives and augur well for the coming years. The following pages will be devoted to highlighting these evolving and exciting changes that, I believe, greatly benefit my future and that of all residents. I join with all my fellow residents in jubilantly celebrating the Tenth Anniversary of my Happy Home. One resident who recently joined our community, remarked, "This place is like one big hug!"

The Big Change

The biggest change to Woodland Pond came about in the spring of 2016. From the time of its construction up to March of that year, Woodland Pond of New Paltz had been a member of an organization known as Health Alliance, Inc., which was the sole corporate member of the organization. Woodland Pond had a Board of Directors that was subordinate to the Board of Directors of Health Alliance in governing our community and, consequently, had very limited authority in decision making and mostly just met to approve motions already passed by the Health Alliance Board.

Effective March 24, 2016, Woodland Pond became a self-sponsored CCRC, renamed Woodland Pond, Inc., and the relationship with

Health Alliance was terminated. This change to a fully independent status was unanimously approved by the Board of Directors of both Health Alliance and Woodland Pond, as well as the New York State Department of Health, Ulster County Industrial Development Agency, Ulster County Resource Corp., and the bondholders holding the underlying debt for Woodland Pond.

Woodland Pond's Board of Directors was now solely responsible for all decisions pertaining to governing the community and overseeing its future welfare. In their new role, one of the first things the members of the WP Board did was to change the bylaws to allow two residents or more (up to a maximum of 20% of the Board's total membership) to join the Board. The notice went out to the community for all residents interested in applying for a place on the Board to submit a resume briefly outlining how their past profes-sional experience and their record of service to Woodland Pond's community might qualify them as a candidate. These resumes were submitted to the Residents' Council who then interviewed each of the candidates and selected two residents, Ray Smith and me, as their choices.

Ray and I were invited to attend the monthly Board meetings in April and May, and at the Annual Board Meeting in June, 2016, we were duly elected to the Board. What was especially interesting about our membership was that, unlike some other CCRCs who had resident board members who had no voting privileges, Ray and I enjoyed full voting rights equal to all other members. I felt truly honored to represent my community as one of the first two resident members of the Board.

Our newly independent Board quickly decided to operate in a different manner, delegating a lot of the work to standing Board Committees that, in turn, made reports and recommendations to the full Board for approval. Thus, all Board members were now required to serve on one or more of these committees, and we even had sub-committees for special areas like planning our Annual Retreat and our yearly goal-setting and self-evaluation.

Given our retirement status, Ray and I volunteered for more than our share of committee work to relieve some of the burden on our fully employed members. We both serve on the Governance Committee and the Strategic Planning Committee while also volunteering to serve on three sub-committees. Ray generously volunteers to serve as recording secretary for the Governance and Strategic Planning Committees while I also serve on the Executive Committee as Board Secretary.

Our first three-year term expired in June, 2019, but we have both opted to continue our Board membership for another three-year term, and have both been reelected for a second term. (The maximum continuous-service allotment is three three-year terms, or a total of nine years.)

One of the earliest challenges I faced in the first several months of my becoming a Board member was that some residents felt that they could bring their complaints about daily community problems directly to me to be addressed. Again and again I had to explain that Michelle was completely in charge of the daily operation of our community and supervising our extensive staff and she should not be circumvented by trying to bring issues to any Board member as this was not our level of jurisdiction.

I consider Michelle Gramoglia to be one of the great blessings to be bestowed on Woodland Pond. Having been the Controller from the day that Woodland Pond opened its doors in 2009, she knows intimately the entire history of our community and, of great importance, its intricate financial underpinnings. In 2013 Michelle was appointed Executive Director; her title was changed to President and Chief Executive Officer in 2016. She is responsible for overseeing and managing all daily operations of Woodland Pond and reports to the Board.

As a not-for-profit organization, Woodland Pond has no stakeholders; the Board provides the governance. However, there is a robust regulatory framework in place that dictates how CCRCs operate, including requirements for budget reviews, rate appraisals, review of contract language and assurance of services provided to residents.

Michelle's interactions with the Board have always been honest, open and forthcoming, engendering a mutual respect and a productivity level that could be a model for any CCRC. She is aware of everything that is taking place within our community, and with her Open Door policy she invites all residents to speak of their concerns directly to her. So often in discussing thorny issues with the Board I have seen her place her first priority on residents' needs and feelings, reflective of her true empathic nature. Like any effective leader, she is always looking ahead to how we must change to keep Woodland Pond competitive and flourishing. And, as you'll see in these pages, we have made many changes to further that goal.

During my many years of professional life, I served on many different kinds of boards, which gives me a standard, I believe, by which to judge the effectiveness of our Woodland Pond Board. When you have board members who need to assert overblown egos and doggedly insist on their opinions and viewpoints over all others, or contentious cliques vying for power, as I have previously experienced, there is not only a significant decrease in productivity but the board atmosphere becomes hostile and sour, discouraging volunteers from serving.

To state it honestly after three years of service, I have never before been a member of a board that works so smoothly, so harmoniously and consequently as productively as our Woodland Pond Board. To date, all members can voice clear and deeply held views but yet there is a group desire to strive for consensus, and I cannot recall when our motions have not been passed unanimously. The respectful and cordial tenor of our interactions makes it a pleasure to attend and participate in all Board meetings, especially when you see the level of commitment that your fellow members, who are not residents and volunteer their time and talents, demonstrate to furthering the goals of Woodland Pond. This, too, I count among my community's blessings.

Our newly independent Board decided to publish copies of the minutes of its meetings for availability to residents. I also offered to write an article for our monthly newsletter on various topics concerning the Board. These lines of open communication have been well received.

2016 Board Retreat

To get our newly independent Board, with its newly elected Resident Directors, off to a fast start, a half-day instructional retreat was carefully planned. The Agenda included an overview of a CCRC's structure (a facility combining housing, services and long-term care) and history (originated from religious and fraternal organizations that provided care in institutional settings). Additional topics included Board Governance and New York State Law, Compliance Roles and Responsibilities of Health Care Boards, Internal Controls and Financial Accountability for Not-For-Profit Boards.

I took special note of two important topics that were introduced. With the dissolution of our relationship with Health Alliance, all legal and governance requirements for Woodland Pond were now vested in its Board of Directors, including: Strategic planning; Health care credentialing; Quality assurance and risk management; Election and removal of Board members; Appointment and removal of corporate officers; Bylaws; Budgets; Changes in services provided by Woodland Pond; State licensing; Contract negotiations; Approval over financial decisions such as debt, expenditures and sales; Litigation; Affiliations; Corporate decisions such as dissolution.

The second topic dealt with the accountability of all Not-For-Profit Corporations to the public, in terms of:

DUTY OF CARE: To act in good faith with that degree of care which an ordinarily prudent person would exercise under similar circumstances, and which you reasonably believe is in the best interest of the Corporation.

DUTY OF OBEDIENCE:

--You must pursue the Corporation's mission;

--You must determine how that mission is best fulfilled;

--You cannot divert resources to other purposes.

DUTY OF LOYALTY:

--Best interest of the Corporation;

--Undivided allegiance;

--Confidentiality;

--Conflicts of Interest (When a Director or Officer, directly or indirectly, has a material personal interest in a contract or transaction.)

This was a jam-packed half-day of important information for all Board members to review, digest and incorporate in their thinking. I believe it also marked the first time that the full scope—and weight—of our new responsibilities were spelled out for us. It had been fifteen years since I had served on my last Board, so this was a strong reminder of the massive range of responsibilities that I and my fellow Board members were assuming. Fortunately, our legal team, present at the Retreat and providing the information on the main topics, also informed us of the extent to which each Board member, acting in good conscience, was indemnified.

A National Conference

In the fall of 2016 Michelle recommended that a member of the Board attend the Leading Age National Conference, an organization that focused on all types of senior housing including CCRCs, which would highlight the latest trends and innovations in this important senior market. She had attended the previous year's national conference and found it very worthwhile but felt it was important at the start of our Board's independent functioning for a Board member to attend and report on what he or she had learned. This year's conference was taking place in Indianapolis and I volunteered to go.

During my career as a school district administrator I had often attended and even been a presenter at national educational conferences, so I was familiar with the very large crowds and frenetic pace of these multi-day events. This conference was no exception. From early morning to late afternoon for four days I packed in as many sessions as I could, often leaving me little time to rush from one session's location to another's. Presentations varied in length from ninety minutes to four hours.

I also tried to schedule time to visit the mammoth Exhibit Hall displaying the latest products geared for senior living (hospital equipment, motorized chairs, electric scooters, walk-in bathtubs, specially equipped vans, call systems, advanced lighting systems, etc.) as well as the numerous booths manned by representatives from companies offering various services (account-ing, architectural, technological, leadership, legal, dining, etc.). While there was a vast range of topics, I naturally selected those sessions that were geared to CCRCs.

From among the thousands of people in attendance at this conference, I was amazed to find only one other resident of a CCRC who, like me, was there because she served on her community's Board of Directors. In attendance were representatives of professional management firms, marketing firms and agencies offering expertise in specialized care-giving areas, e.g. dementia, as well as CEOs of nursing homes, CCRCs, Community Senior Centers and age-restricted senior housing developments; also numerous lawyers, bankers, social workers, nurses and various staff members of CCRCs and Skilled Nursing facilities.

On my first visit to the Exhibit Hall I had a personal incident of discrimination based on either age or lack of authority. In seeking out those booths that I felt might have pertinent information for Woodland Pond, I quickly became aware of how I was being shunted to the side or completely ignored (with a glance at my identity tag and a condescending smile) because I had filled out my badge as Dick Barry, Resident, Woodland Pond CCRC. That night at my hotel, I got a black magic marker and changed my tag to incorporate my former professional title of Dr.

and added Board of Directors. When I returned to the same booths the next day, I was treated like a rock star, showered with attention, inundated with pamphlets and promotional brochures and given small gifts as mementos of my visit. But the treatment I had previously received was a lesson not to be forgotten.

I came away from this informative conference with a sharp awareness of the rapid and dramatic changes that were taking place in CCRCs across the country and how Woodland Pond had to keep up with these changes to maintain a competitive edge or else suffer a decline. Michelle's previous message to the Board and the residents about CCRCs needing to begin refurbishing their community every seven or eight years was right on target with what other CCRC presidents were saying at the conference. But freshening the environment was not enough; whenever possible, we also had to upgrade certain areas like technology to stay competitively attractive.

The big topics that dominated the sessions focusing on CCRCs, which I stressed to my fellow Board members in a lengthy written report upon my return, were technology, the need for a Mission Statement reflecting a community's culture, expanding our sources of revenue, developing a strategic plan for long-range goals with intermediate benchmarks, and exploring affiliation Our biggest challenge seemed to be to continue providing excellent services for our current Woodland Pond population while simultaneously pivoting our marketing strategies to attract the Baby Boomers.

While this conference had outlined for me many challenges for Woodland Pond to tackle, I also came away pleased with all the aspects of our community that seemed outstanding when compared to other CCRCs that I had heard about at the various sessions I had attended. I returned to Woodland Pond and prepared a one-hour oral presentation to the residents on my findings, decidedly upbeat, including the present and projected future state of CCRCs and how national trends could affect our community. Of course, I also prepared a more detailed written and oral presentation for my fellow Board members and Michelle.

I hoped that through my extensive reporting, Board members might gain a wider perspective on Woodland Pond in comparison to other CCRCs across the country in order to have a more objective view of where we currently stood and what we needed to do to improve our profile for the future. I stressed what I had heard again and again throughout my conference days that it was most important for residents to actively participate in working with their management team to effectively bring about change, and noted with pride how Woodland Pond was definitely ahead of the curve in this area and must continue this trend.

So many of my conference's major topics had also been stressed at the previous year's conference that Michelle had attended. Additionally, Michelle served as the Vice President of the Leading Age New York CCRC Council, so she was familiar with the range of activities taking place in the other twelve CCRCs in our state. She and the Board were ready and eager to tackle some big challenges.

Creating A Woodland Pond Mission Statement

I had no sooner returned from the Leading Age National Conference when Michelle engaged the Board in creating a Mission Statement for Woodland Pond. Great emphasis had been made at the conference on the fundamental need for all CCRCs to succinctly state the fundamental principles undergirding their daily interactions and forming their community's unique culture.

The ground rules for a Mission Statement, as I came to understand them, were simple in concept but challenging in execution. It should not be any lengthy document but rather a concise, pithy statement reflecting those values that all constituents—CEO, Board members, staff and residents—shared and were demonstrated in the course of daily life. Driven by values and behaviors of the collective group, it should basically reflect "the way things are done around here." It should be viewed as a fundamental reference point in defining ways for our organization to succeed through strategic planning for the future.

The first challenging steps in forming our Mission Statement were to seek alignment and congruence on the vision of the CEO with the individual Board members' personal values. To my surprise, Michelle led us quickly to conclude that there were no major discrepancies between our organizational values and the individual values of our Board members. Perhaps the voluntary nature of serving on our Board without any monetary compensation reflected a genuine concern for the welfare of others that matched the care-giving outreach of our not-for-profit organization.

The next step was a harder challenge: How to capture the values and vision of Woodland Pond that formed our culture in precise words that rendered a comprehensive profile to which all

Board members, coming from different professional backgrounds, and Michelle could agree.

I had attended a workshop on Mission Statements at the conference in which the participants were asked to write a one sentence Mission Statement for our communities. We were told that our sentence should not be filled with lofty notions but should encompass what our community was as well as what we aimed to be. As a Woodland Pond resident, at that time for five years, I asked myself what had I found exceptional about the culture of my community that made me love my home so much. This exercise proved challenging for me as well as the other participants in capturing the essence of our communities in just one sentence.

On my third draft, I was able to reduce my statement to one sentence. It was this: Woodland Pond is an extended family, active in and outside our community, where all members treat one another with respect, loving concern and the highest standards of care." We had been advised to consider what would appeal to the Baby Boomers (Seventy-eight million Baby Boomers first turned sixty-five in 2011) as the next group of clients for CCRCs; hence the phrase, "active in and outside our community." I also included "highest standards of care" to reflect both a present and a long-range goal. It was my observation about Woodland Pond that many residents, including myself, thought of our fellow residents and many of our service staff as part of our "extended family," and this relationship possibly set Woodland Pond apart from other communities.

I presented my one-sentence draft to my fellow Board members but they chose to go in a different direction, and Michelle wanted to include brief references to staff responsibility and opportunities for personal growth. I readily recognized these areas as being fundamental to the successful functioning of Woodland Pond.

After many hours of deliberation and draft revisions, we finally arrived at a Mission Statement that all Board members and Michelle agreed covered all the bases. Following is that statement.

MISSION:
"Woodland Pond: Opportunity. Care. Connect-ions."

Fundamental Values:
- Personal Engagement
- Communication and Transparency
- Accountability for Actions
- Responsibility for Choices
- Person-Centered Care
- Commitment to Actively Fostering Personal Growth

"All in a safe environment of dignity, honesty, ethical integrity, inclusivity, and respect, enlivened by the natural beauty and cultural richness of the Hudson Valley."

Before this Mission Statement was finalized, Michelle brought it to the staff and residents for their input and approval. Given the high level of resident involvement in all matters pertaining to Woodland Pond, the impressive educational level of residents and the high degree of confidence in speaking their minds—all qualities that enrich our community's culture—considerable discussion and debate ensued before approval was gained from the majority of residents.

In the course of all our deliberations I came to appreciate the symbolic nature of the three carefully chosen words, Opportunity, Care and Connections, and the varied significant meanings they could have for Woodland Pond's different constituencies. As an example, for me the word "Opportunity" can mean the opportunity I have to enjoy a safe, secure environment here at Woodland Pond; or the opportunity I have to serve my community through my rewarding work on the Board of Directors; or the opportunity to speak up on any concern I have about any aspect of my life at Woodland Pond (strictly as a resident and not as a Board member) directly to Michelle or members of her management team; or the opportunity to express my appreciation for the caring nature and excellent service of the staff by filling out Applauds forms and contributing to the yearly staff appreciation fund; or the opportunity to pursue my writing career in the comfort and privacy of my attractive apartment; or the opportunity to make new friends among the shifting parade of residents; or the opportunity to continue to travel and not have to worry about the security of my home; or the opportunity to engage in so many different activities that are offered here; or the opportunity to learn about new subjects through lectures provided here by guest speakers and fellow residents. I could expand further on my list of opportunities but I think I've made my point from my personal perspective.

From a Woodland Pond employee's perspective there are opportunities to advance within our staffing ranks and to receive financial aid in pursuing educational programs that would qualify a person for such advancement. There are opportunities for flexible hours when they meet the needs of both the employee and the employer.

There are opportunities for employees' concerns to be heard through our very active Employee Voice Committee that meets monthly. (More on this committee later.)

For our multi-talented CEO, Michelle faces unending opportunities every day to be creative, caring and controlled in dealing with concerns, emergencies, and any unforeseen circumstance that may arise. Likewise, for our management team, they, too, face no two days alike which offers them opportunities for demonstrating creative leadership.

With the word "Care," too, I find multiple meanings that symbolize what Woodland Pond is all about. Whenever I turn to any member of the staff for help or assistance, I feel that I'm being cared for. I may be asking the concierge to put my copy of the New York Times in my mail folder, or I may be calling on a member of the maintenance crew to install a new light bulb in an overhead fixture (without my having to climb a ladder), or I may be asking Mary Jo Murray, our excellent Wellness Nurse, to take my blood pressure, or I may be asking my housekeeper to give special attention to a spot on my floor, or I may be asking one of our young dining-room servers a question about some item on the menu or asking for chocolate sauce on my ice cream—whomever I'm turning to, I always feel that I am being graciously cared for. But the greatest feeling of being cared for comes from the comfort of knowing that whatever health challenges I might face as the years pass, I will be cared for right here in one of the units at Woodland Pond.

About three months after moving into Woodland Pond, I came down with a bad chest cold and, rather than spread my germs among a susceptible senior community, I stayed in my apartment for almost a week. During that recovery period I was amazed with all the attention I received from my neighbors and new friends from across the community, through phone calls, emails, cards, and assorted baked goods as well as offers to do shopping for me or pick up any medicines I might need. The full impact of Woodland Pond as a caring community was brought home to me during that week of recovery. I felt like the Prince of Wales!

I have witnessed so many acts of kindness between and among my fellow residents that also reflect the care we extend to one another. If you're sick and you own a dog, some neighbor will always offer to walk your pet. If you're sick and you don't drive, even though you can arrange a doctor's visit and be driven in one of the community's vehicles, someone will always offer to drive you in his/her private car. If you're planning a trip that will take you away from home for several days or more, a friend will always offer to pick up your mail and water any house plants you may have. Many residents offer to visit fellow residents assigned to our Skilled Nursing unit (not necessarily their friends), just to offer a friendly hello, inquire how they're feeling and listen attentively to any concerns they might express.

Inspired by such acts of kindness, for a few years until my schedule became too tight, I offered to read to a group of residents with impaired vision who could not read our monthly newsletter and activities schedule. At the beginning of each month I would meet a small group of four or five residents in our beautiful library and I would read the newsletter and schedule to them. They always thanked me profusely, but I felt truly rewarded in making my small contribution to the wider circle of caring that was seen daily throughout our resident population.

I have personally witnessed the great care that Michelle exhibits for our residents. When it comes to weighing the strictest interpretation of some house rule against the feelings or concerns of residents, her decision is always tempered by her deep concern for the residents. She has publicly articulated her view of her leadership role as not being hierarchical based on her authority as CEO, but transactional based on her ability to hear residents' concerns and take measures to respond to them positively. To me, this is the essence of true leadership and the model that I tried to practice in my own professional life as an educational administrator.

Finally, "Connections" also can summon a plethora of symbolic meanings. I feel fully connected to this community because it is the place where I will live out the remainder of my life. I feel connected to my fellow residents because they, too, have committed their remaining days to Woodland Pond and because we share a common general history because of our age category. In my previous book, *Experiencing Woodland Pond,* I devoted a chapter to what I called the Bond of Shared Experience. I began that chapter with the following paragraph.

"With our frequently visiting young families, our young wait staff and the many young members of our administration and maintenance crew, we enjoy a multi-generational environment. However I have discovered a small but rewarding aspect of my life in Woodland Pond to be a social history that we seniors share exclusively."

I then focused on our mutual childhood experience of listening to the radio and experiencing the advent of television, and the major role that movies played in our culture and most of our young lives. The many stars of radio, television and movies of the thirties, forties and fifties are names we can all usually recall with smiles of fond recognition. I made brief references to the Great Depression, World War II, the atomic bomb and the Cold War with Russia, the Korean War, the McCarthy hearings, the Cuban Missile Crisis, the assassinations of President Kennedy, Bobby Kennedy and Martin Luther King, Jr. and the remarkable cultural revolution of the nineteen-sixties.

To younger generations many of these events were things they read about in history books, but to me and my fellow residents they are part of our living history, a connection to the past and to one another in our shared experiences. Nothing starts a more vivid conversation at dinner in our dining room than for some resident to refer to some radio program of the forties or some movie star of that period, and away we all go, flying back in time to add our own vivid memories of personalities or events to the conversation. To me, this is a deep and abiding connection.

I've already mentioned that as seniors we become very attached to many staff members and many of us often look upon our young, caring wait staff with grandparent-like pride. This is a positive emotional connection that enhances our daily life at Woodland Pond but also offers a down side when these young people naturally move on to other jobs and we feel their absence keenly.

Because a strict policy of no tipping of staff prevails at Woodland Pond, residents are given another route to connect with staff in showing their appreciation for all the caring and attentive services they receive, through the Employee Appreciation Fund. By designating an amount of money to be added to the monthly maintenance fee each month or by writing one check in November of each year, the residents, on a voluntary basis, can contribute to this Appreciation Fund. The money collected by these means are then distributed at the beginning of the holiday season to all of Woodland Pond's hourly employees, based on predetermined ratios, and are greatly appreciated by our staff.

Each year, as our resident population grows, the aggregate amount of money disbursed proportionally among employees has also grown. The residents' generosity reflects the strong connection they feel with our great staff.

Our employees, in turn, are deeply appreciative of residents' generosity, and we learn how much this holiday bonus means to them through the comments they write. A few touching examples follow:

* I cried when I opened it (envelope). It helped with grad school application fees, student loans, car repairs, copayments and rent. But it also relieved stress.
* The employee appreciation check came at the perfect time as I needed new tires and an oil delivery for my heat. It really made a difference for me.
* What an amazing blessing your gift has been! We were able to pay some bills, bless a less privileged family and our grandchildren

with gifts. I may even buy myself winter boots.

* I worked a career job for over 25 years and never was gifted like this for any year. Words cannot express our appreciation.

* It helped with a mortgage payment.

* Awesome surprise. I'm a new employee and it gave me great joy when I saw the check. I'm very grateful.

We have another holiday tradition that connects residents and staff and continues to grow and flourish each year. In early December residents are invited to donate furniture and assorted useful household items that they may have brought with them to Woodland Pond but then discovered that they were not needing or using them. This annual drive usually brings forth a lot of furniture, dish sets, cutlery, kitchen appliances, lamps, bed linens, wall hangings, rugs and other useful items that are displayed as part of a Free Store in which employees are invited to select a specified number of items.

Many of our hourly workers find never-used objects as well as gently-used ones and are very happy to get useful things for their homes. One man's discards are another man's treasures, to paraphrase an old saying, and never is this idea as true as in this wonderful tradition of our Free Store. I have donated a set of pots that, because of their original cost, I couldn't bear to part with them and lugged them to Woodland Pond but, since I can only boil water, cook eggs, make toast and turn on the microwave, I never used them. Finally I thought how much more appreciated they would be by some young family and included them in my donations for that year, which also included two new rugs that I had purchased on the internet for my current apartment but didn't like them when they arrived and was too lazy to go to the trouble of returning them. Each December, as I travel around our building, I can hear employees excitedly sharing what they selected from the Free Store and this adds an extra lift to my holiday spirit.

Michelle, as a far-seeing and creative leader, with the full support of the Board of Directors, recognizes the challenges of retaining good staff in a field that is not, for hourly workers, always highly competitive; therefore, she devises ways to induce their connectedness to Woodland Pond beyond, but not excluding, salary scales. Specifically, the following measures have been taken to recruit, retain and maximize our staffing level:

Every department with hourly wage-earners has seen upward hourly wage adjustments;

A retirement plan that includes the sponsorship of a defined contribution tax sheltered annuity plan, covering all eligible employees (Plan). Employees may contribute a percentage of their pretax annual compensation as defined in the Plan and a matching contribution is made by the employer;

New positions have been created within departments to allow staff members to advance themselves and improve their hourly wages;

Additional paid holidays have been added to the work calendar;

After being employed at Woodland Pond for five years, the number of paid days off increases;

Increased spending on tuition assistance in aiding interested staff in furthering their professional development for advanced opportunities within our Woodland Pond workforce;

Increased spending in targeting advertising on line, including a new well-developed social-media-based job posting system targeting hard-to-fill positions;

Significantly enhanced the dollar values of shift differentials for hard-to-fill positions;

Offered more than a dozen options for flexible schedules, where these can be accommodated within departments;

Expanded our modified work assignment program within our workers' compensation program to allow for staff to return to work as quickly as possible, taking into account any physical restraints;

Established a Woodland Pond Care Fund for the purpose of helping employees in emergencies. Expanding on the growing "casual Friday" tradition in the business world, employees were allowed to wear jeans on Friday if they donated two dollars to this fund. When emergencies arise involving financial challenges, an employee can fill out an application that is reviewed by members of the management team and then submitted to a sub-committee of employees for approval;

Expanded our referral bonus program so that any employee in any department who refers a person who subsequently is hired in a full-time position receives a thousand dollar bonus. For less than full-time referrals the employee is entitled to a pro-rated amount;

Participated in a county-wide job fair and met numerous times with the training staff at BOCES.

A superb example of Michelle and her team's creative approach to an acute shortage of CNAs (Certified Nurse's Assistant) is a current trial program to streamline their duties for greater hands-on productivity by shifting certain peripheral responsibilities to the dietary and housekeeping departments and to LPNs (Licensed Practical Nurse).

In addition to these specific enhancements, Michele and her team make great efforts to create an esprit among all employees that demonstrates the great regard and esteem management has for them. The perfect example of these efforts is the annual staff Holiday Party which I have participated in, representing our Board, and have seen first-hand the wonderful spirit this event creates.

One standard solicitation letter from a not-for-profit organization like WP, seeking donations for its hard-working staff is enough to get numerous donations from many vendors. The results are impressive, including several large-screen flat TVs, gold jewelry, bedding and towel sets, wireless headphones, throw blankets, golf bag and accessories, large deep fryer, jewelry organizer, Stanley 75 piece tool set, MacBook Air Laptop, and multiple tickets to major league baseball and basketball games. Employees appreciate the many gift cards, ranging in value from $200 and $170 for two local spas and $100 from Amazon to $50 from Macy's, Kohl's, Best Buy, Visa, Target, Olive Garden, Outback, Panera, to $25 from Dunkin Donuts, Starbucks, Home Depot and American Express.

Beginning in the late morning and extending into the early evening, with a break in the late afternoon, all of the gifts are raffled off (raffle tickets are free), and Michelle is always on hand to see that everything is running smoothly. The PAC (Performance Arts Center) is decorated with a Christmas tree and each department competes in decorating a large, imaginative holiday scene for prizes.

Each department head at Woodland Pond also contributes cash annually to bolster the prize list and contributes toward the very popular all-day "candy buffet." The kitchen staff prepares a dinner of multiple selections and Michelle, the management team members and I, representing the Board, serve the food to the employees as they join the party at various break and lunch/dinner times. Long rows of tables are suitably decorated for maximum holiday cheer to accommodate our large staff as they rotate in and out. In 2018, I stood serving food for over two hours in the afternoon and again in the evening but never felt weary because of all the smiling faces with happy comments that paraded before me.

Throughout the year, a great spirit of fun is engendered for both the staff and the residents when Special Days are declared such as Hawaiian Day or Flapper Day or Baseball Day, and staff members join residents in dressing up to fit some particular theme. In the summer months we've also had outdoor games involving both staff and residents. All these efforts contribute to making real CONNECTIONS.

Of special significance in terms of connections are the many ways that residents remain connected to the world beyond Woodland Pond. First and foremost, of course, is through their families. On any given day I can walk in the public areas of our building and see multi-generations enjoying family get-togethers.

On holidays our dining room is filled with the children, grandchildren and sometimes even great grandchildren of residents, all enjoying a festive brunch or dinner and participating in the holiday spirit as a family. The children of staff members are invited to come to Woodland Pond on Halloween and show off their costumes. Here they can "trick or treat" in a safe environment and get lots of treats and lots of attention from the admiring seniors.

Kindergarten children from the local elementary school are usually given a tour of Woodland Pond on an annual basis and meet residents; some of their questions and comments are priceless. New Paltz high school students frequently have special projects that bring them to Woodland Pond to interact with residents.

For three years I led the discussion groups, open to the public, as part of the One Book, One New Paltz program, when the discussions were scheduled to take place at Woodland Pond. At this annual event, one book is read by folks all across town and open discussions are held at various venues across New Paltz, including Woodland Pond. I found that mingling people of all ages with our residents resulted in a stimulating discussion.

A very special program was brought to Woodland Pond in May, 2019. The New York State Council of the Arts awarded a grant, administered by Arts Mid-Hudson, to Woodland Pond and Barefoot Dance Center. "Embodied Stories" bought together teen members of Barefoot Dance Company and senior residents of Woodland Pond through movement. Special intergenerational movement workshops encouraged participants to explore personal stories, feelings and imagery through dance. A very moving performance resulted from this collaboration.

Each year the residents contribute to a food drive for the college students at SUNY New Paltz. We also contribute annually to a food drive for the Family of New Paltz Food Pantry. At Christmas, we have a "Giving Tree" with the "wish list" for children's presents from local needy families selected by The Family of New Paltz charitable foundation.

Because the residents of Woodland Pond form a significant block of voters and because we are interested and participate in local elections, candidates for the New Paltz Village Board, the Ulster County Executive position and the local Board of Education all come to Woodland Pond to present their views and platforms to our attentive residents. Woodland Pond usually provides transportation on various election days.

The Board plays a role in furthering connections, too. As a resident, when I become aware of some action of an employee or group of employees that deserves special recognition, I draft a letter of commendation in the name of the Board and submit it to the Board Chair for approval. Whenever a resident passes away, I write a condolence letter from the Board to the family of the deceased. Usually, as a fellow resident, I'm able to add some personal anecdotes or comments about my interactions with the deceased. Families, in turn, have expressed their appreciation for this gesture.

In an effort to make direct connections with Michelle's management team, the Board has invited department heads to give brief presentations at Board meetings on what is currently happening in their respective areas and what challenges they see in the future and how they plan to meet them. The Board has also scheduled several social hours with the members of the Residents' Council as a further connection with resident leadership.

For several years I have arranged with the office of the New York State Attorney General to have an Assistant Attorney General visit Woodland Pond and make a presentation to the community's residents on the many schemes that were currently attempting to steal money from seniors. The presenter always said at the outset of his presentation that many of the tricks might seem transparent but the fact was that there were enough seniors falling victim to them to cause millions of dollars in swindled loses.

This point was brought home to me when a particular hoax was described to our residents, but later that year two residents admitted to falling victim to that very hoax. We were also told how to safeguard our personal information and even how to devise better passwords for our network accounts. Playing on seniors' fear, greed or love, swindlers are continuously coming up with new ways to take our assets and we have to be ever vigilant. We will continue to alert residents to new schemes and new safeguards through our connection with the Attorney General's office.

Residents continue to have multiple connections through their frequent participation in activities outside of Woodland Pond. The Wallkill Valley Land Trust sponsors an annual tour of historical houses, and each year Woodland Pond residents serve as docents for that event. The United Way Day of Caring is another annual event in which both residents and staff volunteer in a variety of tasks outside of our community. I know of residents who participate in Habitat for Humanity projects every year.

Many residents belong to different local churches and the local Jewish synagogue and community center, and participate fully in activities sponsored by these religious groups. For example, residents have participated in a Palm Sunday Parade sponsored by St. Joseph's Catholic Church. Other residents attend a monthly luncheon at the New Paltz synagogue. Our nearby Bruderhof Community hosts an evening of dining and fellowship at their home site and sends buses to transport as many residents who wish to attend. This is always a popular event and many, many residents fill the Bruderhof buses.

Residents have even been spotted in the annual New Paltz Halloween Parade down Main Street.

To further enhance opportunities for residents' engagement in activities outside of our community, Michelle recently started a Resident Volunteer Opportunity ("RVO") Pilot Program. This is an outreach program where local businesses, organizations, programs, and individuals in need of short-term volunteer assistance will contact Michelle to inform her of volunteer opportunities for our residents. As of the writing of this book, the program is running for three months and will be extended if successful.

The first offer under this program was from the Huguenot Street Cooperative Nursery School that was looking for volunteers to serve from 9:00 am to 12:00 pm for their Huguenot Street Earth Day 5K and Family Fun Run. (Several staff members were participating in the run.) One of my swim buddies, Annette Johnson, a runner for many years, volunteered to help out at this event and reported to me how much she enjoyed it.

In summary, the multiplicity and variety of connections that I, along with my fellow residents, continue to enjoy both within and outside my community contribute immeasurably I believe, to a full and satisfying life.

Fundamental Values

We (the Board and Michelle) chose to list a set of Fundamental Values as part of our Mission Statement, all of which can be enfolded in our three principal goals of Opportunity, Care and Connections, but simultaneously extend these terms to more specifically define the role of individuals in supporting our mission. Let's take Personal Engagement as an example.

Michelle and her management team make great efforts to instill in all staff a sense of pride, a standard of excellence and individual respons-ibility in contributing to the excellent reputation that Woodland Pond enjoys. Each employee's opinion matters. To reinforce this belief, in 2017 our Employee Voice Committee program was established and remains very active today as a conduit for bringing forth the voices of all employees.

A monthly meeting with management offers the committee's members the opportunity to raise issues of concern that need to be addressed. The prompt response of the leadership team in taking action on issues emanating from employees, demonstrates the team's personal commitment to respecting the concerns of all staff members and reinforcing the concept that each employee can contribute to the betterment of our community.

Management is especially concerned in having residents make connections with other residents and engage with the community and not become reclusive. They recognize that one of the great advantages in living at Woodland Pond for seniors is the continual social interaction that every day can offer. All research on senior longevity points to the crucial role that an enjoyable social life plays as a major factor. While no resident in Independent Living can be forced to sustain a minimum level of sociability, if any resident establishes a reclusive pattern, personal meetings are held with that resident and Sarah Hull, our highly skilled and caring Resident Services Director, to encourage the resident to take part in any community activity, thereby fostering social interactions.

The residents also participate in fostering social interactions among themselves. When a new resident arrives in the community, a Welcome Committee, comprised solely of fellow residents, welcomes them and, without overwhelming them, tries to make them feel comfortable in their new home. Part of this orientation is a mentor program where a member of the Welcome Committee will agree to serve as a personal guide for the first weeks after a new resident's arrival. In these crucial first weeks the mentor can introduce the new resident to the many activities and events that encourage positive social interplay.

Even the Board gets involved in a small way since I try to attend the first social gathering for new residents sponsored by the Welcome Committee and extend official, formal greetings from the Board. In my brief comments I usually encourage these folks to become fully active in exploring all that Woodland Pond has to offer.

The opportunities for Personal Engagement are varied and extensive, as are the variety of ways that the other Fundamental Values listed previously in our Mission Statement can be practiced. As a summative statement we deemed it important to state: "All in a safe environment of dignity, honesty, ethical integrity, inclusivity, and respect, enlivened by the natural beauty and cultural richness of the Hudson Valley." You can see copies of our Mission Statement enlarged on posters adorning walls in our public spaces as a gentle reminder that this is the code by which Woodland Pond aspires to live. The Board was pleased to have worked with Michelle so productively in accomplishing this fundamental task.

A Strategic Plan

Another major task facing our newly independent Board was to ensure, annually, that a long-range plan for the operations and success of Woodland Pond was developed. We focused considerable time and effort on this major project. The strategic plan, itself, was developed with input from all leadership groups in Woodland Pond, including resident leaders and management leaders, and was ultimately the responsibility of the CEO for seeing that it was executed in a correct and timely manner.

Until its independence in 2016, Woodland Pond had never had a strategic plan, nor did its Board have a Strategic Planning Committee. To get started a process for strategic plan development had to be established.

CEO Michelle Gramoglia designed the strategic plan development process to mirror the process used to develop the annual budget. Data was collected from each department head, compiled and translated into a roadmap of activities or goals to be performed and accomplished over defined time frames. Larger economic and operating factors were considered, and the recently developed Woodland Pond Mission Statement was a crucial component. Resident feedback was solicited.

Taking into account all of these considerations, the 2017-2018 Strategic Plan presented a clear vision focusing on providing the opportunities, the care, and the connections that had been identified as the hallmarks of Woodland Pond. The Plan was divided into five categories with priority goals for each category being defined. For each goal, activities to be performed within one, three and five years were identified. A separate series of activities for each goal was defined for the purpose of establishing baseline measures or benchmarks along the time spectrum.

The 2017-2018 Strategic Plan, in executive summary format, follows.

GROWTH

* Financial Growth: Increase cash flow from existing revenue- generating sources, and increase cash flow from new revenue-generating sources.

* Physical Growth: Expand the physical property in one or more areas to allow for growth.

* Programmatic Growth: Foster growth of residents, staff, and waiting lists, through program enhancements.

FINANCIAL STABILITY

* Strategic Financial Planning, Macroeconomic Level: Identify opportunities for access to "safety net" cash flow.

* Strategic Financial Planning, Micro-economic Level: To identify a fixed subset of critical ratios that Woodland Pond will strive to achieve, financially, over a 3 – 5

year period, and to develop an anticipatory framework that assumes a 3 – 5 year accomplishment of each ratio.

QUALITY

* Accreditation: to become accredited by CCAC / CARF and/or achieve equivalent certification at the organization level and the department level.
* Regulatory Compliance: To maintain citation-free regulatory and oversight outcomes.
* Quality Indicators: Establish and maintain a community-wide system of identifying and measuring quality indicators.
* Satisfaction Surveys/Feedback: Establish and maintain a responsive system for collecting feedback on services rendered.

EMPLOYER OF CHOICE

* Compensation: Commit to fair, market competitive compensation and benefits for all staff.
* Training: Enhance training opportunities for all staff and increase related funding.
* Opportunity: Expand non-compensation and training opportunities for all staff.

INFORMATION TECHNOLOGY

* Maximize Use of Existing Assets: Assess and maximize use of existing tech assets.
* Invest in New Technology: Continually invest in new technology.

Our Strategic Plan also addressed capital needs and affirmed a commitment to active succession planning throughout the community. While the above is a summative version, we placed the full version in the Woodland Pond Library. This was, indeed, a most important undertaking, and the Board will work closely with our CEO in updating our plan each year.

Renegotiated Bond Debt

In the final days of 2017, Michelle, our multi-talented and multi-tasking CEO, managed to pull off a near-miracle by renegotiating down the level of interest paid to our bondholders who hold Woodland Pond's underlying debt, incurred to build and open the community. As the days for completing this deal dwindled down to hours, and the Board was holding its breath in deep suspense, hope was draining away.

Then we got word from Michelle of our unexpected good fortune. The renegotiations had been successfully, almost miraculously, completed. With this remarkable achievement, accomplished in literally the last hours of the year before the window of opportunity closed, Michelle ensured that our responsibility for principle and interest payments was reduced by many hundreds of thousands of dollars per year for the next 20+ years.

The Board has always appreciated Michelle's expertise in finance, but never more than in this instance. I personally came to the conclusion that no matter what other talents and background any CCRC President brought to the job, financial expertise was essential. Even with an excellent Director of Finance like Christi Battistoni, working closely with Michelle, the President must understand all financial implications involving any matter before making a decision and taking action. My opinion has been validated by many other challenges regarding complicated finances that Michelle has expertly and successfully guided our community through.

Connected Living

In August 2017, a major technological advancement took place at Woodland Pond. Residents were now seeing large flat-screen television sets on the walls of public spaces, displaying information about the daily life of Woodland Pond that had formerly only been available in print. Now, these screens showed the day's lunch and dinner menus, the schedule for daily activities, special announcements from management, upcoming events, and photos of residents' participation in recent community activities. Other items were gradually added so that we had a digital sign system that posted all the news about our daily happenings that we needed to know.

For the majority of residents who had their own computers, they were given a sign-in code and could now bring up all this daily information at home. Each morning, as I take my cup of coffee and sit down at my computer, before I check for any emails from Michelle or my fellow Board members, or start my morning writing regimen, I always check Connected Living to see what I might like to have for dinner or what event of the day I might choose to attend. I also get great pleasure from seeing the pictures of residents on recent excursions or participating in special events here on campus. Notices of upcoming events can remind me to mark my personal calendar.

Residents and family members who have smart phones can now access all this information directly on their phones. And we now have a "Resident's Only" portal, a moderated message-sharing board for residents to exchange information on a community forum.

Whenever I engage in my morning ritual of information retrieval, I'm usually mindful of the great emphasis placed on improving a CCRC's technological base that was made at the two national conferences I attended in 2016 and 2018, and I always think proudly how quickly and steadfastly Michelle has led us to vast improvements in this area.

In December 2018, Woodland Pond took another giant step forward in introducing an in-house closed-circuit television station (channel 1340). Residents could now sit in their apartments or cottages and see any event or speaker emanating from our Performance Arts Center (PAC) on their television screens. Then in May 2019, another innovation was introduced to our community when Michelle made her first broadcast from her office to all residents via channel 1340, discussing several topics that residents had brought to her attention.

An additional advantage of having channel 1340 was that it could be used to communicate all ALERT notices to residents, informing us of any and all information of immediate importance. If residents had any questions about a fire alarm activation, impending storm, disaster warning, etc., we could turn to channel 1340 to obtain the most current information provided by our management team.

A public room that had originally been set up as a billiards room and used for that purpose by only a handful of residents, was converted in 2018 into a Classroom, replete with long tables and new chairs for group meetings. The Classroom was technologically equipped to be able to transmit on a large flat screen any offering from the PAC. Now, whenever there was an overflow crowd in the PAC, residents could watch what was taking place via closed circuit in the Classroom as well as in their homes. The technology also had the capacity for Michelle to participate in Classroom meetings from both her home and her office. The Classroom quickly became the hub for much activity including Residents' Council meetings, Board of Directors meetings and many committee meetings, and the advanced technology available to us for these various meetings was both used and appreciated. We were clearly marching vigorously into the future, with the forward-looking Michelle leading the way.

To accustom residents to all these changes, technical support was frequently offered. While the role of technology supervisor or coordinator was not part of his job description, Jason Irish, a most affable and knowledgeable young man, quickly became the go-to guy for specific questions or problems we (or even the administration) might be having in managing all the new ways of communicating. Residents also called on fellow residents who were known to be "techies" and, in typical Woodland Pond fashion, both Jason and our knowledgeable residents graciously offered assistance whenever possible.

Students from our local high school even got into the act. In October and November of 2018, special times were set aside for them to volunteer their technical expertise to residents. They were available to provide troubleshooting and technical support for most electronic devices, including help with hardware and software, as well as give guidance in basic computer and smartphone skills. The hours they spent at Woodland Pond went towards community service hours for their National Honor Society applications. After their visits I heard a number of residents rave about these youngsters' degree of expertise and how helpful they had been, but I suspected that the residents were also enjoying the social interaction with a much younger generation, as they always did.

As senior citizens we are all aware that young people have learned their technological skills the way we, as children, learned to ride a bike or hit a ball: it came naturally to us as part of our maturation process. Now, we are learning highly technical new skills at a time in life when learning isn't as easy for us as it once was, and we appreciate all the help we need and can get. Fortunately, here at Woodland Pond there are many hands reaching out to offer us assistance.

As residents we now have so many different ways of keeping pace with community developments beyond a mere printed bulletin. We still have the Chanticleer, our weekly printed news sheet, and Woodland Life, our monthly newsletter so expertly assembled by our inexhaustibly creative Activities Coordinator, Gretchen Daum. We also have a phone number (256-5729) that we can call each morning for the day's schedule of activities and dinner menu. But we can also obtain this information and more by signing on to Connected Living on our personal computers or looking at the large Connected Living screens in our public areas.

When a meeting with the management team and CEO is scheduled, as well as a community meeting sponsored by our Residents' Council, we have the option of attending these meetings in person in the PAC or watching them on channel 1340 in our homes. The only restriction to viewing rather than attending these meetings is that while we can hear everything that is being said, we cannot contribute our own comments. Given the rapidity with which our technology has been advancing, maybe this will soon be possible as well. At least, that's my fantasy. We've advanced so far in such a short amount of time!

Michelle's innovative weekly addresses to the community via this closed circuit television channel is still an additional example of using technology to foster improved communication. We have also recently acquired the capability of showing streaming Netflix films in our PAC so that as soon as current movies are available to Netflix after running in theaters, we can see them.

While I am definitely not a "techie" by nature, I see the many practical advantages of using expanding technology to improve our everyday lives, and I'm grateful that our CEO provides strong leadership, with the ardent support of our Board, in keeping Woodland Pond moving forward in this vital area.

LGBTQ Commendation

A singular honor was bestowed on Woodland Pond when our skilled nursing facility was named a "Healthcare Equality Index LGBTQ Healthcare Leader by the Human Rights Campaign Foundation. Nationally, for 2018, Woodland Pond could boast of being the only such skilled nursing facility as part of a continuing care retirement community that had achieved this highly coveted honor. This designation was the result of marrying the highest levels of hospitality and long-term care with inclusivity for all its residents, staff and stakeholders.

Michelle was delighted with this honor. In a press release she was quoted as saying, "Woodland Pond at New Paltz values inclusivity and person-centered care fundamentally, and the fact that we have accomplished what no other continuing care retirement community in the country has, is testament to our commitment to offering the most welcoming and supportive environment for retirees and long-term care residents."

The Board of Directors was equally enthusiastic in its response. In a formal letter of congratulations addressed to Philip Mehl, our seasoned, charismatic Long Term Care Director, and Diana Briggs, our skilled Licensed Practical Nurse, we noted the special significance that "in reviewing Woodland Pond's submission to be certified as an Equality Leader, our Health Center received a whopping score of 100%."

This designation was achieved with the participation by members of all departments of the community, including Human Resources and Marketing. Policies had to be strengthened, all staff members trained, marketing messaging made clear, signage posted, and much more. This was a multi-month project, and one that Woodland Pond intends to undertake annually into the future.

Philip Mehl, the champion of this effort, spoke eloquently as follows: "We have a diverse population of residents, staff, and guests, many of which openly identify as members of the LGBTQ community. We want to publicly embrace and support the needs of these residents through our person-centered care approach, but also for their neighbors that may privately identify as a member of the LGBTQ community. Every resident and staff person should feel fundamentally supported regardless of how they identify themselves and regardless of whether they have come out."

Philip continued: "Being able to demonstrate to our staff, residents, and visitors that we are committed to actively embracing and supporting the care needs of residents in the LGTQ community is absolutely crucial to me, and to our leadership team as a whole. It was not enough for us just to be able to demonstrate these commitments in the skilled nursing environment; through the process of applying for "Healthcare Equality Leader" status, we made sure that our policies, programs, training, and supportive messaging have been ingrained into every aspect of Woodland Pond."

An unfortunate stereotype of my older generation is that many of us lack an understanding or empathy for LGBTQ people, based perhaps on little or no exposure and just plain ignorance. Let's face it: in our youth and young adulthood years, which all took place before the 1969 Stonewall riots, homosexuality was not a topic discussed in homes or portrayed on television or movies, or ever discussed in polite society. The crudest descriptions (fag, faggot, fairy, bull dyke) were indicative of the scornful condemnation that society decreed for anyone suspected of such tendencies.

Because my former wife was a professional ballet dancer, and, in that era, the ballet world was largely composed of gay men, I came to know a lot of them and their stories at an early age—I was dating my future wife when I was twenty. I learned to understand and appreciate many aspects of their lives in, what was for them, the very turbulent 1950's era: they were condemned by society as a whole and mostly ostracized by their families; they were often persecuted both by straight citizens and relentlessly by the police; no one encouraged them to form lasting one-on-one relationships except their own basic needs for love, trust and committed companionship, just as straight people felt these needs; the notion that they preyed on children was totally false since that was a separate category of pedophilia which they heartily condemned; they did not make advances to people who were not gay; they were not all effeminate or identifiable by specific traits. For what they suffered and endured I came to have much respect for them; for their boundless resilience I came to admire them. For the bonds of friendship I formed with some of them, I came to trust them.

In coming to Woodland Pond I was greatly surprised by the total acceptance of LGBTQ people by a majority of residents—supposedly my unenlightened generation—and soon learned that this attitude was based on the fact that in the 21st century so many of their children or grandchildren, friends or neighbors and even spouses had come out of the closet and been completely accepted and fiercely loved. Having been born and lived as an adult in Manhattan, and attended two of its liberal universities, NYU and Columbia, I was very comfortable with a heterogeneous, polyglot, multiracial, sexually diverse population and was happy to discover at Woodland Pond that openly LGBTQ community members were fully integrated and warmly appreciated among our staff, residents and Board of Directors.

Coincidentally, while writing this section on the topic of our LGBTQ award, a newsletter crossed my desk from the National Continuing Care Residents Association in which an article featured a lesbian couple who were suing a mid-western CCRC for refusing them admission to its community. The article quoted the couple as saying, "They are committed to continuing their lawsuit as they want to ensure that same-sex couples are treated with dignity and respect in continuing care retirement communities nationwide." My immediate thought was that they should have applied to Woodland Pond where they'd enjoy both dignity and respect plus a whole lot of caring and affection.

It was purely intentional when we highlighted "inclusivity" as a key word in composing our Mission Statement. I feel that this special honor bestowed on Woodland Pond was truly earned and truly warranted, and that our emphasis on inclusivity serves as a beacon of welcome to all people regardless of race, religion, ethnicity, sexual orientation or gender identification. The only thing I personally find intolerable, like many of my fellow residents, is intolerance.

Artists Front and Center

I have always been awed by the number of resident artists here at Woodland Pond and the impressive works they produce. I have even purchased several paintings from two fellow residents and have them, along with the painting of a third resident that was a gift, prominently displayed in my home. Our Performance Arts Center (PAC) offers a continuously changing display of residents' works, and our Art Scope Committee has created wonderful opportunities for individual residents to showcase their artwork. Well attended evening events give the artist a chance to talk about his/her work. I've enjoyed seeing exhibits of oil paintings, pastels, pen and ink sketches and a show of fiber arts. In addition, the Art Scope group has offered monthly movies and videos about artists such as Van Gogh, Vermeer and others. We've also had a display of artwork created by Woodland Pond employees, clearly a talented group.

A casual stroll around the hallways of our Independent Living wing offers additional proof of our residents' artistic talents since many of the displayed paintings have been done by residents. While my talents don't bend in this direction, I've been able over the years to purchase paintings and donate them to Woodland Pond for decorating our halls. Each resident has the option of decorating the area immediately surrounding her doorway; to walk down any corridor and see the variety of work displayed definitely adds, I believe, a homey touch to our environment reflecting the individual personalities, tastes and creativity of our residents.

An annual event that draws a larger public crowd each year is our Kaleidoscope of Arts show in the fall. At this day-and-a-half long event, open to the public, the full spectrum of residents' creative efforts is always on display: pottery, ceramics, quilts, books (including mine for the last six years, with a new book each year but one), jellies and jams, knitted and crocheted hats, scarves and gloves, paintings (oils, water colors, acrylics) photography, photo cards, jewelry, woodcarving (including furniture and birdhouses) and most likely other items that I've forgotten.

A half day on Friday is given to browsing by our staff and a full day on Saturday from 10 am to 4 pm is open to the public. The PAC is transformed into a market place as residents man tables on which their products are displayed. Residents rent a 4 by 8 foot table for $20, but can keep the money from the sale of their products, although some donate their proceeds to our Benefit Fund. Adding to the festive air is a bake sale in our Art Studio, organized by Vivian Yettru, with all home-made goods donated by residents; and in the hallway outside the PAC several gift baskets are displayed, the contents of which are also donated by residents and invitingly arranged by Joan Kleinegris, Kathy Kelly and Vivian Stoner. These baskets of assorted goodies are raffled off at the close of the show on

Saturday. All monies from the bake sale and the raffle go to the Woodland Pond Benefit Fund (more on this later), and I'm always surprised each year at the hundreds of dollars that we net.

I always feel a special surge of pride when I'm sitting at my book table, signing books and conversing with New Paltz neighbors, but primarily because I'm surrounded by my fellow residents representing the great scope of talents thriving in our community. In an environment where arts and crafts are honored, publicized and displayed, we seem, unselfconsciously, to stimulate and encourage one another to continue our efforts in pursuing creative outlets.

We are especially proud of a recent accomplishment by a celebrated artist among our residents: Trina Greene, a native of the Philadelphia area who studied painting at the Boston Museum School but considers herself a self-educated sculptor, had, in 2013, completed a bronze statue of an eleven-year-old Sojourner Truth, the African-American abolitionist and women's rights activist. The statue was called

Isabella, which was Sojourner's real name before she changed it, and now stands in Port Ewen.

Trina thought that the Isabella statue would be her last, but she was very moved by the recently discovered history by a local historian of the thousands of men, women and children who died in the Ulster County Poorhouse during its existence from 1828 to 1972, many in mass graves, without benefit of headstone or commemoration of any sort. From all those deaths during all those years only one remaining grave marker was discovered in 2000; it was that of Rebekah Brower who died in the Poorhouse in 1852 at age thirty. The tombstone was inscribed with four moving stanzas of verse, each ending with the refrain, 'Who'll Weep for Me."

On May 15, 2019, a formal unveiling of Trina's life-size bronze statue, *Aging Woman,* took place in the presence of local dignitaries and many Woodland Pond residents. Of special interest to us was the fact that a much loved fellow resident, Annette Finestone, had, at the age of 97, posed as Trina's model for this statue, but, sadly, had recently passed away at age 102. The statue, along with the Brower headstone, is permanently displayed on a landscaped patio with seating for contemplation, adjacent to the land where the Poorhouse stood, and dedicated to all those forgotten souls who died with no one to mourn or remember them. Artists, like Trina, never seem to lose their zest for the next creative project, which is inspiring to all of us who also enjoy exploring our creativity.

A New Benefit Fund

With Woodland Pond's independence from Health Alliance, we now had to establish a separate fund for specific purposes wherein donations would be tax deductible. After careful investigation by residents and management of different ways of establishing this fund, it was designated as the Woodland Pond Benefit Fund (the Fund), a charitable fund maintained with the Community Foundations of the Hudson Valley for the benefit of Woodland Pond.

The Woodland Pond Benefit Fund Committee was organized to administer certain activities of the Fund. It was a joint committee of members of Woodland Pond's management team as well as our CEO, and residents approved by the Residents' Council.

The purposes of the Fund were specified as:

*Staff Education Scholarships: To provide financial support to employees seeking higher education and vocational training.

*Program Development: To provide funding for the physical, cultural and intellectual enrichment of the residents.

*Physical Plant Development: To provide support for projects designed to enhance the physical Woodland Pond community.

There are several ways that residents and their families can donate to the Fund:

*Directly by the resident:
Check or credit card donation; As a tribute to or in memory of a loved one; By naming the "Woodland Pond Benefit Fund" as the beneficiary of life insurance, IRA, or other retirement plan proceeds.

*<u>With Woodland Pond Staff Assistance</u>:

Designation of all or a portion of a resident's Woodland Pond entrance fee refund to the "Woodland Pond Benefit Fund" through the Business Office.

*<u>With the Assistance of a Financial Advisor</u>:

Through donations of securities and closely held stock—avoid capital gains taxes and receive a tax deduction of the fair market value of the donated assets; Through Required Minimum Distributions (RMD's) from an IRA; Donations of real estate or other marketable assets.

*<u>With the Assistance of Legal Counsel</u>:

Creation of a resident's bequest via the resident's estate plan or will.

Because of my personal circumstances of having no living family, my will specified that my assets were going to NYU and Columbia University, in appreciation (and payback) for their giving me full scholarships and graduate fellowships with living stipends to complete four degrees. However, my nearly eight years at Woodland Pond had allowed me to function in such a blissful state of contentment, security productivity and happiness that I resolved to leave money in my will to establish a scholarship fund for the Pond's hourly workers, with the restrictive clause that the employee had to be pursuing a degree (AA, BA, MA, etc.) or a certification conferment at an accredited college. In this way I felt I was passing forward the generous educational opportunities that had been afforded to me when, as a high school dropout, a veteran and a married man with children at age 25, I decided to pursue higher education to improve the financial security of my family.

With the generous assistance of the staff at Community Foundations of the Hudson Valley, Michelle, our ever obliging CEO, and Brigitte Blum, our knowledgeable Director of Human Resources, we hammered out a detailed scholarship plan that, while managed by Community Foundations, was established as a separate entity.

Employees who successfully completed two semesters with scholarship funds were to be listed as Dr. Richard V. Barry Scholars in a formal commemorative listing to be established in some public space at Woodland Pond, as designated by Woodland Pond's President.

Residents were to serve as executors of this fund and were to be selected by the Residents' Council and formally announced to the CEO in January of each year. Each resident executor could serve for four years. An executor's responsibility was to see that all the provisions of this plan were carried out, but s/he had no role in the selection of the successful applicants. Management had the responsibility of publicizing this scholarship fund to employees in July and January of each year.

I calculated that the limit placed on tuition reimbursement ($4,000 for two semesters) would equal the historically <u>minimum</u> average yearly return on the Community Foundations' invest-ments, which therefore should fully replenish the total amount of money in my separate fund. In this way my scholarship fund should last for many years as a token of my great appreciation of all the young hourly employees who contributed immeasurably to my happy years at Woodland Pond. I was thinking particularly of the dining room servers who often started working here at sixteen and demonstrated such kindness, courtesy and, above all, patience with us seniors to an extraordinary degree. They always won my respect and affection.

As a means of growing our Woodland Pond Benefit Fund quickly, I had suggested to Michelle and to Anne Gordon, the Residents' Council liaison to our Board of Directors, that we might start a One Hundred Club. My idea was to publicize an opportunity for residents to **pledge** to donate $100 (one hundred dollars) every year to our Fund and be listed, either by name or as anonymous, as a One Hundred Club member on a formal list to be displayed somewhere in our public area.

My idea seemed to gain everyone's endorsement, and a campaign was soon launched, resulting in a good number of residents (but not, to date, one hundred residents) making a hundred-dollar donation. However, somewhere between my articulating this idea to the powers- that-be and the execution of the idea, the concept of "pledging" to continue donating that amount each year got lost, or perhaps it was intentionally dropped. Still, I'm pleased that we made a good deal of progress in enlarging our Fund and perhaps in future years the notion of "pledging" will be revived. I'd be the first to sign the pledge.

Food, Glorious Food

From my personal perspective, the food here at Woodland Pond, which always satisfied my palate, has only gotten better over the years. Having made that statement, I recognize that any time a group of seniors come together over a meal, there is bound to be a variety of opinions about the food, and that is certainly true at Woodland Pond. With our individual dietary restrictions, our mandatory monitoring of salt intake, our comparing all dishes to how we used to make them (if cooking was our specialty), our favoring spicy or plain food and our desire for small or large portions, our dining room on any given night is filled with residents questioning our ever patient and courteous serving staff.

During my years at Woodland Pond I've seen a good amount of turnover in the dining supervisory staff and our chefs, but within the last few years we have enjoyed stability with Ronnie Licata, our dedicated General Manager of Dining, Keri Ciastko, our diplomatic Operation Manager for Services, and Alaina Cancel, our friendly Dining Services Assistant. Their scope of responsibilities can best be understood by numbers: 600 meals served daily (including all three units of the Health Center and Independent Living), 80 employees and 5 managers.

This is a team that is very responsive to residents' concerns, complaints and suggestions and works cooperatively with the residents' Dining Committee under the effective leadership of Joan Kleinegris, its seasoned Chair. Additionally, Ronnie and Keri are continually seeking ways to improve the general dining experience for all residents. For example, when a survey revealed that the majority of residents did not like the Sunday brunch served buffet style, we switched to sit-down table service.

I can honestly claim that I always have a choice at dinner that appeals to me. The main reason for this ever appealing selection is the expansion of our Pub Menu that offers a wide variety of hot and cold sandwiches, wraps, hamburgers, pizza made to order, salmon, chicken and a variety of entrée salads. If I don't care to select one of the three entrée offerings on the Dinner Menu, I just glance over to the left where the Pub Menu is placed within the leather folder and find a suitable and tasty substitute.

For me, personally, the most exciting innovations centering on food services have been the expansion of offerings in our Pub. It may be the Pub at 4 pm when residents exuberantly enjoy Happy Hour, but now, for the major portion of the day, it's become the Woodland Café from 8:30 am to 3 pm. For each day of the week there is a breakfast special and a lunch special, along with a soup of the day. I'm partial to the Broccoli Cheddar Soup on Monday, the Tacos on Tuesday and the Sausage, Egg & Cheese on a Biscuit breakfast on Wednesday, but all the daily offerings are tempting.

To complement these choices, the Café offers the complete Starbucks coffee service: coffee, five flavors of espresso, cold Macchiato, Latte and Cappuccino, and a variety of flavored syrups to customize any drink. Before the Introduction of Starbucks coffees at Woodland Pond, I had resisted the lure of these drinks; now I've become an addict.

Between 10:30 am and 3 pm, an added attraction are the Smoothies, fresh 16 oz. blended fruit drinks that are a great healthy snack and are offered in five different flavors, one for each day of the week.

Another exciting change took place in the spring of 2019 when the Pub/Café area was open on Sundays for the entire day (8:30 am – 8 pm). Offerings now included a continental breakfast and, of course, Starbucks delicious coffees, while lunch consisted of soup and smoothies, and a hot dinner option was offered from 5 pm – 7 pm. All these offerings were in addition to our sit-down brunch in the dining room. Residents were clearly delighted with these new options they had on Sunday, including the chance for more socializing.

The choices that residents make in their dining habits are as varied as their responses to food. Some residents only come for lunch and are seldom seen at dinner time; others, like me, come only occasionally for lunch and come for dinner during the week but not on the weekend; still others prefer to cook a lot of their meals in their apartments or cottages—that's why we have fully equipped kitchens—and seldom appear in the dining room; and then there are those who come daily for lunch and dinner and the brunch on Sunday.

Entrees at dinner time are frequently offered in a regular portion or a lighter portion for a reduced price. Since many residents opt not to eat desserts, they are offered for an additional price to the complete dinner which includes soup or salad, rolls and butter, entrée with choice of two sides, and soda, coffee, milk or tea.

A recent innovation introduced by Michelle was a change in our meal plan. Instead of having a set amount of money allocated for meals for each month which, if not spent at the close of the month, was lost, now we could carry over any balance on our meal plan allowance from month to month, up to the end of the calendar year. I find that this helps my budgeting process because if I'm planning to have several out-of-town guests for dinner at some future date, or planning to host some celebratory dinner party with my resident friends, I can conserve my meal allowance money one month and build up a larger sum over several months for these future special events.

It's always comforting to remember that whenever I am sick, I can call Mary Jo Murray, our caring and award-winning Wellness Nurse, who alerts the kitchen staff, and I can have my meals delivered to my apartment at no extra charge.

Michael, our new head chef, has impressed residents by leaving the kitchen and mingling with residents during dinner time to listen to their comments and concerns. He and Ronnie Licata have previously worked together and are a good team. He has already introduced some new menu items that have been well received by residents.

I acknowledge that I am rendering one man's opinion about the food at Woodland Pond, which I continue to find very satisfying. That doesn't mean that I don't occasionally follow the advice of the dining supervisory team and return a dish to the kitchen that, for whatever reason, doesn't satisfy me. But I'll hasten to add that on the rare occasions when I resort to this tactic, the immediate response is to correct whatever I'm complaining about. This positive approach empowers residents to be participants in improving our overall dining experience. It's an evolving process but on an upward trajectory.

Special Events

A brief glance at one of our weekly calendars can indicate the great variety of activities and events offered to us at Woodland Pond. A resident could be engaged from early morning, starting with the informal coffee group that meets in the pub at 7:30 am, throughout the day and into the evening, ending with some cultural offering in the PAC after dinner: a movie, lecture, art exhibit, dance recital, chamber music ensemble or presentations by local political candidates. But there are special events that really stand out in my memory.

For the last six years Woodland Pond has hosted the Rambling Rose Fashion Show, and for the last three years I have served as the MC of this event. Rambling Rose, a local ladies' clothing boutique, dresses up to eight or nine volunteer residents in current fashions from the store's collection, including hats, scarves and jewelry. Our maintenance crew constructs a long "runway" in the middle of the PAC for our models to parade on, and seats on either side of the runway are always filled with cheering, clapping and whistling resident-spectators, a sell-out crowd.

For this event, to add to the lively and fun-filled atmosphere as the resident-models really strut their stuff (and dance and skip and sway and undulate) down the runway to the beat of loud disco or rock-n-roll music, I usually prepare some extravagantly exaggerated remarks as each model begins her walk. For instance, I might say: "She's had a celebrated career as a history professor but her fondest memories are when, as a young girl, she ran away to join the circus and cleaned up after the elephants." "Before moving to Woodland Pond, she had a thriving career as a lady wrestler." "She's the only woman who ever said No to Porfirio Rubirosa." "She's a star of stage, screen and bachelor parties." If these remarks seem wild and weird, they have to be judged in the context of the evening's focus on rousing fun, and they always seemed to get belly laughs from the audience. I hope I'm asked back for a fourth time as MC, for this is an evening when residents are really at their unguarded best and I enjoy being part of this exciting scene.

Another memorable special event for me was an Antique Auto Show that was held right here in the parking lot of Woodland Pond last year. Reconditioned cars, mostly from the 1950's, were displayed in all their shiny chrome extravagance that marked cars of that era. A small music ensemble played as folks strolled among the beautiful autos. Many residents, especially the men, saw cars that were either duplicates of, or closely resembled, the cars that they owned as youngsters.

A palpable wave of nostalgia swept across the parking lot as residents shared stories of the cars of their youths. Prospective residents had been invited to attend this show, and, after viewing the cars, proceeded to our Pub where free ice cream sodas were being served. The weather had cooperated and the sun was spotlighting the beautifully restored cars. Their owners were available to answer any questions, but residents mostly wanted to swap stories with them. All the smiling faces and animated conversations attested to the success of this event. I think we are planning another auto show in the fall to coincide with our tenth anniversary celebration. Great!

Another memorable recent event for me was of an entirely different nature. When I first heard that Death Café was coming to Woodland Pond, I thought it sounded like a goon squad that was going to hasten our departure into another world. I overcame my repugnance at this unfortunate title when I read the following description.

"A Death Café is a gathering of people who eat cake, drink tea or coffee, and confidentially have conversations that break the taboo of talking about dying and death. People often leave feeling 'connected,' 'uplifted,' 'fulfilled,' 'thankful,' and 'informed.'

"A Death Café is not a bereavement support or grief counseling setting. It may not work for people who are not able to discuss death comfortably and openly."

I knew there were residents for whom a Death Café would not be a suitable setting. These were the same residents who found it very challenging to accept the death of a fellow resident, even if the deceased had been of a great age upon dying. I understood that the passing of any resident was a reminder of our own mortality, which can be a frightening or depressing thought.

I was eager to participate in the Death Café because my response to witnessing the demise of a fellow resident had an opposite effect on me. It certainly did remind me of my own mortality, but that realization made me cherish each and every day that was still mine to enjoy; an incentive to live each day consciously and fully. So rather than become depressed, I became energized to engage with daily life as actively as possible and be thankful for whatever time was still allotted to me.

The residents who joined me at the Death Café expressed various, sometimes antipodal views about dying and death, but the fact that we could share and discuss our attitudes and feelings with others seemed, indeed, to result in an uplifting experience for most, if not all, participants. Many were guided by religious beliefs while others, like me, regarded these experiences merely as part of the natural cycle of life affecting all things. We listened intently and respectfully to one another and came away thankful for such a forum that allowed an exchange of ideas on an extremely important but sensitive topic for seniors. While I wish the organizers would find a less alarming title for these gatherings, I will certainly attend the next Death Café that comes to Woodland Pond.

Dedrick's at the Pond

During my years of residency I have always used a local pharmacy called Dedrick's, located on Main Street in New Paltz, for my prescription drugs and over-the-counter health aids, as well as small gift items and holiday decorations. This pharmacy always seemed to me to be like a small-town drug store (minus the soda fountain of my youth) where I, as a customer, was given individual attention. My prescription drugs were on file there, along with a credit card. Whenever I needed a refill, I just called the store in the morning and by the afternoon, the prescription would be delivered to our concierge desk.

I was delighted to hear that Dedrick's was opening a satellite store at Woodland Pond, and this became a reality in December 2018, when

Dedrick's at the Pond opened for business, not just for residents but for the wider public as well, with hours Monday through Friday 10 am -3:30 pm, and Saturday 10 am – 3 pm. Staff, families and residents were able to place a credit card on file and thereafter needed only to tell the clerk their names once the card was on file, in order to make a purchase. Since I already had a credit on file at the main store, I did not need to re-file my card. Cash and checks were also accepted.

Due to legal restrictions, a pharmacist could not be on site at the Woodland Pond store, but all prescriptions ordered by phone or in person at the main store would be delivered to the Woodland Pond store and picked up there. Susan Stanmyer, the very pleasant and responsive clerk at our store (and daughter of resident John Fracasse) calls me whenever one of my prescriptions is available for pick-up.

I fell easily into the habit of dropping into our new satellite store several times each week and picking up health-care items. Since the store also offered ice cream, soda, candy and assorted snack food, the temptation to pick up one or two of those items was irresistible. I have heard several lady residents say that they have purchased small gift items, greeting cards, scarves, jewelry and even pocketbooks at the store, so it seems that Dedrick's at the Pond is off to a successful start and residents appreciate the shopping convenience it offers.

As a 501(c) 3 not-for-profit corporation, Woodland Pond is required to ensure that no more than 5% of the total square footage of our property is used for non-mission-related purposes. The spaces used by Dedrick's at the Pond, Ulster Federal Credit Union, our two hair salons, our medical doctor's office and the dentist's office (both used for private practices) are all included under this cap. The convenience of having all these services available on campus cannot, in my estimation, be overstated.

Additionally, we have a volunteer retired optometrist who comes to Woodland Pond once a month to make minor repair on eye glasses for FREE; a local CPA, also a Woodland Pond Board member, who brings a huge shredder compacter to our premises for residents to dispose of unwanted files; the local police department comes to pick up any unused prescription drugs; and most recently we now have a massage therapist who will come to our homes for a varying fee depending on the amount of time we choose for a massage.

At the monthly Complimentary Happy Hour sponsored by Woodland Pond (distinguished from the daily Happy Hour organized by residents), we recently welcomed a musical duo who play live background music while we socialize. Their repertoire includes jazz hits form the Great American Songbook as well as blues and other popular songs, performed on a 12-string guitar and electric bass. Thank you, Susan Griss and Larry Bush, for adding an extra happy dimension to our Happy Hour.

With so many people catering to residents' needs, is it any wonder that we feel pampered?

Making a Difference

I am constantly reminded of what a caring community I enjoy here at Woodland Pond, and some special examples immediately come to mind.

Vivian Stoner, a good friend, has, over the course of her long-time residency, initiated many things that enrich our lives. She discovered a very attractive curio cabinet in the basement, brought it up to our lobby and, with the approval of the administration, started a program of having residents display samples of their interesting private collectables for a month. I participated with small sculptures, kachina dolls, hand-painted tiles and sand paintings representing the art of southwestern Indian tribes. Other exhibits have included Christmas objects and collectible dishes. Each display is accompanied with a printed description by the owner about the collection. The lighted cabinet sits next to the front entrance in the lobby and delights many visitors.

Vivian was also responsible for starting a series of yearly dances at the Pond. At these events she serves as an enthusiastic DJ, using her own music tapes to keep things hopping. She supervises the transformation of our PAC into an inviting night club with small tables topped with lamps and a portable wood dance floor. Vivian also started Bingo games and serves as the announcer. She bought and donated fish and a water-spray for the two small ponds in our courtyards, which many of us found very enjoyable to watch. She serves on the Décor/Design Committee, assists other residents with their displays for our Kaleidoscope of the Arts show and volunteers as a model at our annual fashion show. She even organized a holiday party for the residents on her hall. Her zest for life is boundless, and her contributions to Woodland Pond are ongoing and continually impressive.

Another resident, Jean Hicks, has for years carried out a project that has brought joy to so many of our residents in our Skilled Nursing unit. Jean made arrangements with local funeral homes to deliver floral arrangements, after a funeral, to her. She then rearranges them into small bunches and places them in donated vases that she has gathered from across the community, and has them delivered to the patients in Skilled Nursing. Woodland Pond's Board of Directors recently sent a letter to Jean, commending her for these repeated acts of thoughtful solicitude.

Ray Smith, my fellow resident-director on our Board, and his wife Anne have, during their years as members of Woodland Pond's community, been bringing their two therapy dogs, Anzac and Diggy, Australian cattle dogs, to our Health Center every week to offer comfort and cheer to those residents who like dogs. And many of them do. Anne and Ray also self-published the much praised book, *Wartimes Remembered*, a collection of thirty-seven stories dealing with our residents' wartime memories and experiences during WW II. This fascinating book is available in our library and can be purchased on Amazon.

What I found especially interesting about these histories of my fellow residents was how many of them were teenagers when they entered the service during WW II and then took advantage of the G.I. Bill to attend college and start their professional careers, marry and raise a family. The statistics from the late 1040's through the late 1950's indicate a significant increase in American's "middle class," and that seems clearly to confirm that the government's educational support to veterans had long-term benefits not only for the veterans but for the nation's economy and potential for future growth. G.I. mortgages also contributed significantly to the growth of home owners in our country, which became another measurement of our growing middle class. Many of our WW II generation have passed away since they told their stories. This book, however, is a fascinating read and we owe a large debt of gratitude to Anne and Ray for their patience and skill in self-publishing it for Woodland Pond.

When Suzanne Orchowski joined our community, she was already an accomplished dulcimer player. In typical fashion, a good number of our residents wanted to learn how to play this instrument, and a group of them was soon performing on their dulcimers as part of our Pondaliers' performance. Suzanne was a member of a long-established dulcimer group outside of our community and arranged for them, too, to give a performance at Woodland Pond. Thanks to Suzanne, dulcimer players are now an established resident group, adding an additional musical dimension to our pleasure.

Resident Pat Kirkpatrick is really an unsung hero who is ever helpful to so many residents but never broadcasts his caring for the needs of others. Whenever I'm away for any length of time, it's Pat I turn to for collecting my mail, or driving me to the local train station in Poughkeepsie. When my car's battery was dead on a freezing winter's day, it was Pat whom I called on to give me a boost. No matter what his fellow residents ask of him, as long as he is available, he graciously and generously helps in whatever way he can. Pat is a prime example of the caring nature of so many residents who are always willing to extend themselves to assist their neighbors.

I think an outstanding example of one person caring for another came from my own experience a few years ago. For some conflict in my schedule I was not able to participate in our annual Kaleidoscope of the Arts show. When I mentioned that regrettable fact to my friend Kathy Kelly, she suggested that I set up my table with my various books on display and since her table was directly opposite mine, she would handle any sales at my table as well. Considering that she had the largest collection of hand-made objects of any resident, I thought this would be a very challenging task but she convinced me that she could handle it.

When I returned to Woodland Pond at the end of the day of the Kaleidoscope, Kathy presented me with an envelope representing the sale of over sixty books. I was flabbergasted! She treated the whole subject as though it was no trouble at all. That's a caring friend! I know I treated her to dinner the next night but that seemed small recompense for such a generous and thoughtful act of kindness.

This is just a small sampling of residents' contributions in forming the caring community that is Woodland Pond. There are many, many more, and I feel that this communal spirit of giving cannot be captured in any pamphlet or article on Woodland Pond and has to be experienced in our daily lives to be truly appreciated as part of our unique profile. Remember what I previously quoted one new resident as saying: "This place is like one big hug."

Benefits of CCRC Living

An incident occurred a short time before I began drafting this book that I believe captures the benefits of life in a community like Woodland Pond.

Michelle, in an effort to extend detailed information about our community to key professionals in our area, had arranged a luncheon for financial planners, accountants and attorneys. At this event she planned to provide an overview of Woodland Pond to these men and women and the services and security we offered to any senior clients they might have. She had invited me to attend the luncheon as a member of the Board and I gladly accepted.

The attendance of the invited guests was good, and Michelle delivered a concise, comprehensive picture of our CCRC status and what we offered. What emerged, to my surprise, during a Q &A session was how little any of these professionals had previously known about Woodland Pond, or the underlying concepts of CCRCs in general, so it quickly became clear to me that this was a most worthwhile outreach effort on Michelle's part.

On that particular day, the forecast was for sun during mid-day, followed by increasing clouds in the early afternoon and several inches of snow expected by late afternoon. Why this weather report is important to my story will, I promise, become evident.

I had been relatively silent during most of the luncheon, adding only a few comments from the perspective of a resident when I thought they were appropriate. Then, as the discussion was winding down, an accountant opined that while everything about Woodland Pond seemed most attractive, the real stumbling block for his clients was simply that they were not ready to leave their homes, even if they were elderly and finding home ownership an increasing burden. My head perked up and I gave the accountant the following response.

Before coming to Woodland Pond, I lived in a three-bedroom, two bath, upscale condominium situated on top of a 180 foot bluff that offered me a panoramic view of the Long Island Sound and, on a clear night, the lights in the towns that dotted the shoreline of Connecticut. If I was still living there today, with the weather forecast that has been given for accumulations of snow this afternoon, I would be eating a frozen dinner, alone, in my condominium.

I continued with my response. Because I live in Woodland Pond, I will leave my apartment, meet friends for dinner in our dining room and have an enjoyable two-hours of relaxing socializing before strolling a short distance down the hall to attend a musical performance in our Performance Arts Center. I don't have to worry about the furnace in my condo—in a back-porch closet partially exposed to the elements—going out, or shoveling the snow off my entry porch and steps when the snow stops. Tomorrow morning, instead of shoveling out my car and driving several miles to my gym in order to fulfill my daily regimen of swimming laps, I will walk down my hall to our beautiful indoor, heated pool and do my laps.

I concluded my monologue with: This is just one small example of the difference between continuing to struggle with home ownership and living in Woodland Pond. There are many others.

It did snow that afternoon and I did exactly what I had described I would do, being grateful once again for my CCRC life style.

Our Health Center's Stellar Achievement

Woodland Pond can boast of a very significant achievement: For the last five years our Health Center's Skilled Nursing unit has received a five-star rating from the federal government's Centers for Medicare and Medicaid Services, the highest rating a CCRC's skilled nursing unit can receive.

A very elaborate, extensive and quite complicated evaluation system is used to arrive at a rating ranging from 1 Star (lowest) to 5 Star (highest). The broadest categories, with many subsets, are:

* On-site Health Inspection ratings including multi-year surveys;

* Quality Measures ratings (with ten Quality Measures—seven for long-stay chronic care and three for short-stay, post-acute care);
* Staffing Ratings: To earn 5 Stars on the Staffing rating, the nursing facility must meet or exceed the Centers for Medicare and Medicaid staffing study thresholds for both Registered Nurse and total nursing hours per resident day.

The evaluation criteria were recently changed and strengthened, resulting in a reduced number of skilled nursing facilities across the country receiving a 5 Star rating, but Woodland Pond sailed through the new rating system with the same highest score for the fifth consecutive year. On average, only one of every five skilled nursing facilities receives this outstanding rating.

Woodland Pond's Board took note of this meritorious achievement and wrote the following to Philip Mehl: "We should never become so complacent that we take this singular designation for granted and not recognize the consistent and concerted efforts on the part of all the Health Center's staff in earning this top evaluation for both long-term care and shorter rehabilitation stays year after year."

This distinction serves to underscore Woodland Pond's profile as a premier Continuing Care Retirement Community, along with the other accolades we receive and the excellent word-of-mouth reputation we enjoy.

Work Order Refinement

Mention the subject of work orders to any group of residents and, like the subject of food, you'll get a variety of responses. Tom Tango, our dedicated, experienced Director of Plant Operations and Security, would be the first to acknowledge that the work order system can always be improved, but let's give credit for effort.

A recent set of procedures for residents' work orders was developed by Tom with the Physical Plant Committee, comprised of residents, and approved by the Residents' Council. It outlined in clear, precise terms how to put in a work order, what information should be included in the work order, how to check on the status of a work order, and what process is followed once a work order is placed in the system.

A work request is placed in "Worxhub" an interactive software program that is used to record, assign and track residents' work orders. Noel Perry, our efficient maintenance coordinator, determines what needs to be done, and the work order is then assigned to the maintenance technicians on their digital tablets. The status of the work order is updated on these tablets as appropriate. The types of status are: completed, pending, or waiting for a part.

What both Michelle and Tom have stressed to all residents is that work orders are assigned on a priority basis as follows:

* Life/Safety – Anything relating to the life-safety systems, or items that would impact on life/safety (example: beeping smoke detector, door does not open properly, exposed wiring, problems with fire detection system or sprinkler system);
* Corrective Maintenance – Something is broken and needs to be repaired to function properly;

* Requested Maintenance – Nothing is wrong but an item is requested (example: hang a picture, move furniture, install a shelf);
* Preventive Maintenance – Items that, if done, greatly reduce Corrective Maintenance (example: change filters, check doorknobs, change batteries).

We now have a dedicated Preventive Maintenance technician, which reduces orders for Corrective Maintenance. We have also added a Heating and Air Conditioning technician, which reduces orders for corrective measures with our individual heating and a/c units.

Residents can go to Worxhub to learn the current status of their work orders.

This is a summary of the detailed outline on how residents can successfully submit and follow up on their work orders, which was distributed to the community. In this area, too, we've improved the work order system through an innovative use of technology.

Learning Never Stops

Woodland Pond is always a beehive of activity, and that includes an increasing number of opportunities for learning. Many of our residents are members of the Lifetime Learning Institute, and some of the Institute's classes are offered right here at Woodland Pond.

If you would like to learn how to play (or brush up on) chess or mah jongg (or join a poker group), how to square dance, how to make a quilt or crochet a scarf, how to paint, how to make pottery, how to write a memoir, or to brush up on your French, Spanish, Italian or Yiddish, you've come to the right place in joining our Woodland Pond community where active learning is certainly a hallmark of our resident population.

Any resident can offer to start a new program and see how the other residents respond. And management is always receptive to finding a place for a new program. A glance at our monthly calendar of daily activities attests to a crowded schedule from which a resident can join as many activities as s/he feels comfortable with, or perhaps you want to learn about some new subject that is being offered on a trial basis.

On-going discussions groups focusing on books, current events, matters of faith, bereavement, politics and other concerns, offer ample opportunities for full participation and learning from a wide divergence of opinions. Our numerous resident committees are never static but are usually looking for new members, and committee work is a sure way to learn more about our community. The Chairs of our various resident committees give annual verbal reports on their respective committee's accomplishments to date at community meetings.

What I find impressive about our community is the number of residents who are willing to share their expertise, gained from decades of professional experience or the pursuit of a hobby, with presentations to their fellow residents. Then we have all our artists, many of whom are willing to share their development as painters, sculptors or writers and their methods of stimulating their creativity. This sharing of knowledge and experience among residents forms a special unifying bond that adds to the oft-repeated notion that we are an extended family.

Our outstanding staff is also willing to make helpful presentations to residents. Rob Dunn, Director of Environmental Services, has told us all about recycling and composting. Christi Battistoni, Director of Finance, expertly delivers quarterly reports on our current financial picture. Recently Susan Kaufman, our staff dietician, made a presentation on salt in our diets and plans more lectures in response to the positive feedback she received.

Before assuming the responsibilities and time commitments inherent in my work as a member of the Board of Directors, currently serving as Board

Secretary, I found by joining several activity groups and volunteering on a number of committees (mostly in succession) that I was learning a great deal about my fellow residents as well as the subject or topic at hand and also honing my skills at working with others to arrive at a consensus. Given the educational and intellectual levels of our residents, the pursuit of mental and creative stimulation is constantly and vigorously pursued at Woodland Pond.

What always impresses me about my fellow residents is that some of us may not be in the best of health and we may use canes or walkers or electric scooters, but that should **never** be misinterpreted as paralleling a lack of mental acuity. Two of the sharpest minds I ever experienced in my eight years of residency belonged to a lady and gentleman who were over one-hundred-years old when they recently passed away, and their quest for knowledge and stimulation never abated until the last weeks of their lives.

When I first came to Woodland Pond, I was seated at a table in the dining room and watched as a couple, seemingly considerably older than I and progressing unsteadily with the aid of walkers, approached my table and joined me. My bias that this would be a dinner of dull, desultory conversation quickly faded as they engaged me in a lively, wide-ranging discussion of political, societal and personal topics, leavened with a good amount of humor. I thoroughly enjoyed myself and drew an important lesson from that night's experience, reminding me of the old adage not to judge a book by its cover. For me the lesson was not to judge my fellow residents by their physical frailties as representing any loss of mental sharpness or vast interest in the world beyond Woodland Pond.

New Delivery Service

In a previous section of this book I've outlined many of the technological advancements that have come to Woodland Pond to enhance our lives. Most recently we were introduced to another use of smart technology.

A grocery delivery system called Peapod allows residents to use a smart phone, computer or tablet to order groceries and have them delivered right to our kitchens. Now we can skip the trip to the store and let our fingers do the shopping. The details of this program were explained by resident Deborah Moore, and residents with physical challenges have already found this to be a convenient way of shopping.

Recycling Efforts

The residents of Woodland Pond are clearly interested in saving our planet from being overwhelmed with garbage, but for me, and, I suspect, for many others, recycling has been a subject that has definitely been an ongoing learning experience. But thanks to the leadership of our knowledgeable (and patient) Director of Environmental Services, Rob Dunn, I think our community has made great strides in refining our recycling efforts.

Rob created large, three-dimensional posters illustrating the various items that should be recycled and those that should go into the trash. He outlined what batteries needed recycling and educated us about the numbers inside the triangles on the bottom of plastic containers. Over time, certain guidelines changed and Rob always kept us informed of these changes.

Eventually we started recycling kitchen waste in composting bins: one at the back door of our south wing and one at our north wing's back door. Bulletins were distributed across the community outlining what should be composted and what was not suitable for composting. This is an informative itemized list that I am continually consulting to be sure I'm depositing the right objects in the composting bins. We now have a separate receptacle for paper and cardboard products.

Sometimes, as I deposit items in the recycling bin, I will see items that do not belong there, which indicates to me that this is a subject in need of constant reinforcement. Still, we have come a long way as a conscientious community, eager to do our part in keeping our planet healthy for future generations.

Another National Conference

For the second time as Woodland Pond's Board of Directors' representative, I attended the 2018 Leading Age National Conference, this time being held in Philadelphia.

An estimated seven thousand people attended, with nearly five hundred exhibitors, over four days. To give an impression of the scope of participants who see the senior population as a burgeoning field for marketability, in attendance were real estate developers, management firms, rehabilitation firms, architects, lawyers, CEOs and CFOs, nurses, start-up company reps., food service reps., builders, accountants, numerous companies representing the latest technology, furniture company reps., specialized vehicles reps., banking reps., and board members of national organizations catering to all types of senior living: age-restricted apartment buildings for independent living, assisted living apartment buildings, nursing homes and CCRCs—encompassing both not-for-profit and for-profit organizations.

During my four-day attendance at the conference I met only one person, among the thousands in attendance, who was a CCRC resident and member of her community's Board of Directors We happened to be seated together during a luncheon offered in the Exhibit Hall. After the usual introductory pleasantries, the lady who came from a southern state, started asking me pointed questions about the operation of my community.

We discovered that we both had young women serving as our CEOs, and I was asked how my CEO got along with the Board. Of course, my response was enthusiastically positive about Michelle's productive, proactive and open relations with the Board. Then the lady asked me if there were any factions within my Board that hampered or completely obstructed decision-making, resulting in strained relations and unproductive meetings. I replied, again with enthusiasm, that among the current thirteen members of our Board, cogent, informed discussions and debates could take place, but there was a synergistic effort to reach and respect consensus, and our formal motions for action were consistently passed unanimously. I added that during my active professional life I had served on many boards but none quite matched the Woodland Pond Board for open, respectful interactions among Board members and between the Board and our CEO, thereby enhancing everyone's efficiency in achieving desired goals.

As I responded to the lady's questions, her noticeable frown deepened and finally she said, "I think I should leave my community and move to yours." Then she told me a dysfunctional tale of woe. Her young CEO was fairly new to her job and while energetic, resourceful and popular with the residents, she seemed reluctant to share any arising community problems with her Board in fear, this lady speculated, of jeopardizing her position. Unfortunately, Board members had other connections within the CCRC and would then confront the CEO, forcing her into a reactive, defensive posture. Among the Board members there were two camps that were openly hostile to each other and always pursuing different agendas, resulting in contentious meetings, behind-the-scenes plotting and a poisonous atmosphere.

I listened attentively to the lady's litany of troubles at the leadership level of her community and left the luncheon feeling blessed that Woodland Pond was singularly free of such challenges to a smooth, productive operation.

At another sit-down luncheon I heard some interesting facts:

* By 2036, the projection is that the U.S. will have seventy-eight million seniors and seventy-six million children under eighteen;
* An estimated two million older adults are experiencing abuse in their own homes;
* Ten thousand new Baby Boomers are retiring every day;
* Official years spanning Baby Roomers are 1945 to 1964;

* Fifty percent of households over fifty-five have no retirement savings;
* Baby Boomers are often becoming the second generation of CCRC residents, but their expectations are vastly different: A variety of meal plans; big gyms; many connections with the wider community; frequent intergeneration interactions; a continued focus on social justice.
* The title Life Plan Community continues to replace Continuing Care Retirement Community, especially with new communities in the west, to signify active years of productivity planned independently by each Baby Boomer resident and facilitated by the management and community.

At the same luncheon, a presenter told the story of a dog named Lucky. A new neighbor visited the family next door and met a friendly dog with only three legs, one eye and missing hair from a bad skin condition. The dog's owner mentioned that the dog also had a bad heart and a kidney condition. "Why would you call the dog Lucky?" asked the new neighbor. "Because," the owner replied, "he's damn lucky that we love him." The moral of this story was for seniors to recognize all the current lucky or positive aspects of their lives and not dwell on the negatives.

One of the most interesting sessions I attended focused on planning vibrant senior communities of the future by using Maslow's Pyramid of Hierarchy of Human Needs as a model for stimulating residents' continuing growth and as a tool for marketing services to consumers. A brief overview, in simplest form, of Maslow's pyramid was presented.

Abraham Maslow, a psychologist, working with college students, postulated in 1943 a pyramid of hierarchy of human needs depicted in the form of a pyramid with our basic needs being the largest part of the schema, at the pyramid's base. The pyramid consists of five components that determine our motivations for our behavior in a specific order; we can only progress to the next level once the needs from the bottom have been met.

* Lowest Level: Physiological Requirements—our physical needs—air, water, food, rest, health;
* Second Level: Safety Needs—absence of fears from surrounding environment, security in shelter, safety from people;
* Third Level: Social Needs—strong sense of belonging through family, friends and/or community, with help received and reciprocated;
* Fourth Level: Esteem Needs—a sense of self-satisfaction through good self-esteem, power, prestige or recognition;
* Fifth Level: Self-Actualization—once all the other steps have been met, this last step allows us to express ourselves creatively and grow to our full potential.

In reviewing this pyramid leading to the highest level of self-actualization, I was struck by the realization of how I and many other residents at Woodland Pond must have had all the needs of the previous four levels met in our safe, secure and stimulating environment in order for so many of us now to be pursuing our creative talents.

At another session about leveraging wider community connections, the presenters stressed the importance of appealing to the next generation of CCRC clients by maximizing connections with outside agencies and businesses and creating intergenerational environments. At the end of this presentation, audience members were invited to contribute what their senior complexes were doing in terms of bringing in activities from outside the community.

I was happy to speak of Woodland Pond's interactions with the Life-Long Learning Institute's program, our participation in the annual One Book, One New Paltz community read-and-discussion groups, our recent auto show, our eye glass repair program, the Ulster Federal Savings Union branch and Dedrick's Pharmacy branch on campus, our Mohonk Preserve passes, our Ulster

County Communities Fund, the elementary and high school children who do special projects with our residents, our hosting local political candidates to amplify their platforms, our monthly birthday parties sponsored by the local Shop Rite market, our annual Kaleidoscope of the Arts featuring arts and crafts products and open to the public, our music recitals featuring local artists, our hosting play-reading presentations by local acting groups, our hosting a local business group's monthly dinner meetings, our arrangements with our local public library for delivering books on tapes, our hosting presentations by local LGBTQ groups, and our annual fashion show.

This recitation all came pouring out in a quick cadence and at the end I was almost out of breath, but I received a spontaneous round of applause from the other participants.

This was, for me, a most stimulating and rewarding, illuminating and exhilarating confer-ence. For every session that I attended and heard of current trends and recommended new practices for CCRCs, I took note with both pleasure and pride of how Woodland Pond was rapidly changing in some big and some subtle ways: vast technology changes including our becoming part of Connected Living and our new technologically advanced classroom, our own closed circuit television channel for broadcasting events directly to residents in their apartments, and the computerized system for servers to place lunch and dinner orders; the installation of LED lighting around the campus; recycling and composting improvements; new day-long food service in the Pub during the week and on Sundays, with continuous resident input on dining choices; new contract types for entering Woodland Pond; the 5 Star rating our Skilled Nursing unit received for the last five years; our precise but comprehensive Mission Statement and the five-year Strategic Plan developed by Michelle and our Board of Directors. All of these advances will, I believe, keep us on the cutting edge for attracting future residents and advancing the welfare of our community.

I found that my attendance at two Leading Age National Conferences provided me the opportunity to compare Woodland Pond to what's new and exciting in the senior housing industry, which lent objective reinforcement to my subjective view of my community's excellence. I was delighted, once more, to return home and report my findings to my fellow residents, Michelle and her management team and my fellow Board members, convinced that, within our physical limitations and financial restraints, we were doing everything possible to sustain our reputation as the premier CCRC in our region.

Our Concierge Service

I cannot celebrate the joys of living in Woodland Pond without mentioning the remarkable, supportive services performed by our dedicated, conscientious ladies (and one gentleman) who are the heartbeat of our community and man our concierge desk.

They are the first persons visitors see and usually interact with, upon entering our main entrance, or the first voice that is heard when calling Woodland Pond's general number. The services they perform for residents are numerous and varied, which make our lives that much more comfortable. I often see new residents at the concierge desk asking a question about some aspect of our daily lives—Woodland Pond is a complex society with a lot of schedules and offerings and guidelines to learn for those just joining us—and invariably the concierge has a suitable or reassuring answer.

For me, some of our personnel at the concierge desk represent a stable presence throughout my eight-year residency. Lisa Ceo was the first smiling face that welcomed me to Woodland Pond on my first exploratory visit here, and she is still smiling when I see her now. I don't think I have ever gone to her with a question that she was not able to answer or get an answer for me in a matter of minutes. She is a marvelously reassuring presence in my daily life.

Jeffrey Seitz began working at Woodland Pond as a server in the dining room when he was sixteen, following in the footsteps of his two older brothers, Simon and Harrison. (His younger brother, Samuel, completed the quartet by also joining the staff at sixteen.) Interested in writing and familiar with my books, Jeffrey would politely ask me questions or seek my advice about writing, and I was happy to encourage a budding writer. At some point Jeff applied for an opening at the concierge desk and was accepted, where he has applied the same courtesy, diligence and solicitude to his new tasks as he displayed in his previous assignment. He is now finishing his master's program at SUNY New Paltz, and I, along with many residents, have watched his maturation and noted his accomplishments with delight. Jeff is also a talented pianist and has performed several one-man concerts for our very receptive community.

To demonstrate the thoughtfulness of our concierge staff, let me share what I've experienced with Denise Peterson who is at the concierge desk on the weekends. I subscribe to the New York Times on the weekend but do not always leave my apartment too early on Saturday and Sunday. Sometimes there's a shortage in the number of Times delivered to us and since I want to be sure to get my copy, I was in the habit of calling Denise and asking her to put my copy in my mail folder behind the concierge desk. I did this for only a few weekends after she joined the staff and then, making my usual call one Saturday, she cheerily told me that she had already put my copy aside. She has followed this practice regularly since then, and I marvel at how she can remember this small detail in the midst of all the hurly-burly that typically surrounds her desk. But she does!

Whether it's long-term people like Lisa and Jeffrey, or newer members of our concierge staff like Aly, Kathleen, Joni-Marie and Ashley, their smiling faces, warm voices, cheerful personalities and eagerness to be helpful, adds still another comforting, supportive dimension to my life at Woodland Pond, an amenity I usually associate with high-priced apartment buildings, and one that all residents should greatly appreciate.

Our Extraordinary Marketing Department

Our marketing department, which for years has consisted of two extremely talented, creative and dedicated women, Shannon Scaturro, Director of Marketing, and Denise Kennedy-Shane, Marketing Coordinator, is a great example of what a dynamic duo such as these two ladies can achieve through hard work, diligent follow-up and creative sales approaches. I believe a most important aspect of their success is the individual attention they give to each prospective Woodland Pond resident, and the gentle guidance they provide in steering them through the hurdles of decision-making, house selling, moving and settling in.

Prospective residents are offered a "30-Day Pass" to Woodland Pond, which means that they can participate in our activities, use our facilities and even enjoy some meals, in order to give them a full experience of what their lives would be like in our community. If they're active and enjoy hiking, we also offer them (and all current residents) day passes to the beautiful, vast Mohonk Preserve.

Every spring Shannon and Denise invite prospective residents to a luncheon at which a panel of current residents share their stories of why they chose Woodland Pond and what they see as the advantages of CCRC living. This panel is mainly composed of couples with one or two singletons and me representing all the people who come here as widows or widowers or a few divorced men and women, as is my case.

In my remarks, I always stress that I came to Woodland Pond knowing no one or nothing about the Hudson Valley, but was taken with the extraordinary natural beauty of the area surrounding this community and the diversity of New Paltz as a university town. I liked its convenience in getting into Manhattan for cultural events. I was very impressed on each of my five investigatory visits with the smiling greetings and friendliness of the residents whom I casually encountered, and the patient and thorough answers that management gave to all my numerous questions.

I go on to say that I had done a lot of research on CCRCs and had visited four other ones, but Woodland Pond kept calling me back. Finally I saw a two-bedroom, two-bathroom apartment that had extra side windows because it was at the end of a corridor and afforded me magnificent views of the Shawangunk Mountains and even the Catskill Mountains and endless green acres of preserved land.

I tell my audience that what finally hooked me into signing on the dotted line were two things: (1) the realization that Woodland Pond was the only CCRC I had investigated that offered single occupancy in their Health Center rooms—one of my top requirements; and (2) when I filled out the worksheet comparing ALL my current expenses in living in my up-scale condominium complex (including $100 a week for my housekeeper, and a lot of gym fees for my daily regimen of lap swimming, and special assessments for repairs and upgrades to my complex), I discovered that my monthly maintenance on the Woodland Pond apartment I had selected was only $200 more than my total current bills, and felt that this extra cost was well worth the many additional services I was getting for that one fee.

I try to stress in my remarks how lucky I feel in retrospect that I came to Woodland Pond while I was still young and healthy enough (74) to take advantage of everything that Woodland Pond had to offer in the way of activities, committee work and excursions, and how I was free to pursue my second career as a writer without so many of the burdensome chores of daily life that I had to face before moving here.

I like to end my comments by telling my audience that after eight years of living at Woodland Pond I have my own personal meaning for the acronym CPR. For me it means that I feel CONNECTED to a community of vital, vibrant and caring people; I feel PROTECTED from the vagaries of the future by knowing where I'll be for the rest of my life and, thanks to Life Care, I'm protected from vast financial changes if I have to avail myself of any of the three units in our Health Center; even occupying an Independent Living unit I feel an extra measure of protection with the Personal Emergency Response System (PERS button) that I can wear around my neck and summon help in any emergency by pushing the button, or feeling protected with the management's policy of a follow-up evening call when a resident has not been seen by the staff during the day; and I feel RESPECTED by both our management team and my fellow residents for my volunteer work as a member of our Board of Directors (nominated by our Residents' Council) and the author of two books detailing my joyful living at Woodland Pond.

Because the couple who bought my condo-minium also bought all its furnishings, I was able to start from scratch in furnishing my Woodland Pond apartment and purchased everything in an appropriate scale for the size of the rooms. I admit that I also spent lavishly in adding many upgrades to my designated apartment before I moved in, including crown moldings, wood floors, granite counters, glass-brick back-splash, side-by-side refrigerator, kitchenware storage garage, deep sink with special faucet, ceiling fans in the main rooms, twenty-one hi-hats in the ceilings throughout the apartment, five new ceiling light fixtures, dimmer controls on all wall light switches, customized window treatments throughout, hand-painted mural on half-wall separating kitchen from living room, higher toilet, glass shower door and a glass-enclosed porch.

With my work as a writer and my work as a Board member, I spend a good portion of my day in my apartment, and I have never regretted the money I spent on making this apartment my ideal home. Shannon likes to bring prospective residents to see it, with the understanding that this is not the basic model but rather what you can do with a unit to make it exclusively yours. She has also arranged for a videographer to film my apartment for a more convenient way of showing it to future residents.

Marketing used my book, *Experiencing Woodland Pond*, detailing my experiences in living at Woodland Pond after two years; they gave it to serious prospective residents. Based on the response that Shannon, Denise and I all received, people felt it was helpful in learning about Woodland Pond from a resident's perspective, including how and why I came to Woodland Pond. Now, six years later, I'm bringing my history up to date, following a casual suggestion from Michelle that it would be nice to have a current version for Woodland Pond's 10th Anniversary Celebration. When I reflected on how many important changes have occurred at Woodland Pond and how often I've been a participant in those changes, I was strongly motivated to get to work with a new book that I hope marketing will also find to be helpful to prospective residents.

At the end of 2018, the great news was that, thanks to the unstinting efforts of our energetic

Shannon and Denise, we had exceeded our projections for end-of-the-year occupancy totals and now had only three units available. Of equal importance was the extent of the wait list for units involving future residents who had already made a down payment on a particular unit size. With careful and patient follow-up of prospects, our dynamic duo now had a long wait list for units. Full occupancy is the life blood that keeps any CCRC healthy, along with a reassuringly long wait list, and Woodland Pond was enjoying excellent health.

Resident Survey Results

Michelle and her management team are eager to survey residents to ascertain their degree of satisfaction with how things are going for them at Woodland Pond, to address areas that are not meeting a group standard of satisfaction, and to consider suggestions for improvements. The positive news is that, despite our considerable increase in population over the last two years, our latest survey of residents found an increase in the level of overall satisfaction when compared to the most recent survey of a few years ago.

I personally attribute this satisfaction upswing to the way Michelle makes herself available to all residents. She has even set aside specific time during the week when residents can sign up to speak privately to her, and at other times they can just drop in if her door is open and she is available.

Also, the Residents' Council has an EARS program that invites residents to air their concerns and suggestions for improvement to the Council. Based on this input, as well as residents' comments made directly to individual members of the Council, a running Concerns List is kept regarding all areas that the Council feels rise to the level of a community issue and warrant attention.

Michelle values this list and reports to the Council at least once a month about the progress her staff has made in remedying the issues enumerated on the Concerns List. Through this open and easy communication method—residents to Council and Council to Michelle and Michelle back to Council and then Council reporting to residents in community meetings—we, the residents, feel that we are actively participating in continually improving life at Woodland Pond.

Concluding Thoughts

First, let me share some happy news. On May 22, 2019, Michelle was elected President of the Leading Age New York Continuing Care Retirement Community Council, encompassing all the licensed CCRCs in New York State. This is truly a reflection of the high respect she has earned from her fellow CCRC leaders (she previously served as Vice President), and I feel it also reflects their acknowledgement of the sterling reputation enjoyed by Woodland Pond under her leadership.

Another happy personal note: On June 6, 2019, Ray Smith and I were elected by our fellow Board members to serve a second three-year term on the Woodland Pond Board of Directors. I was also elected to serve again as Board Secretary and, in that capacity, will be a member of the Board's

Executive Committee. We will both continue our work on several committees and sub-committees, which will keep us very busy, but I regard this work as my contribution to Woodland Pond's continued welfare.

As we celebrate our 10th Anniversary of Woodland Pond's receiving its first residents in September, 2009, there is, indeed, much to celebrate. Many changes have been made that, I feel, have contributed to strengthening our community profile for the benefit of both our current residents and for the residents of the future. But I wish to end with the same thoughts I wrote in my previous Woodland Pond book because they sum up everything I believe to be true.

In writing this brief (and, with apologies, occasionally discursive) history of my eight-years as a resident of Woodland Pond, I must stress that these are personal viewpoints offered voluntarily to pay tribute to the residents, staff and administration, all of whom contribute immeasurably to my daily state of total contentment. Despite my ongoing blissful state, I have no wish to present Woodland

Pond as a Utopian society where harmony reigns and conflicts never emerge. No one who has arrived at a senior status would accept that depiction as anything but a fantasy. (I will forthrightly confess that there are three or four residents with whom I cannot stand even being in the same room, but, remember, that's out of a population of about 250 residents in Independent Living.)

I will state, therefore, that while this community turned out to be the ideal place for me, there are a few residents who seem soured on everything and appear incapable of deriving any genuine pleasure from life's daily happenings in their present environment. They often remain remote from the general population and our cheery hurly-burly, or they join groups only to cast a pall over any proceedings with ongoing negative comments. I found them easy to spot in the midst of our happy clan because they seldom or never smile. Fortunately, they are vastly outnumbered.

Experts in the field of gerontology say that as we get older, our fundamental personalities don't change; our basic traits just become more pronounced. Thus, I can only conclude that these few people have always viewed the glass as half-empty rather than half-full. Whatever painful life journeys have apparently caused them to see everything through a negative lens, I feel sad that they cannot embrace their dynamic, gregarious neighbors and be nourished and enriched by this caring and joyful community.

When friends of my age or a little younger visit me and see my happy state of mind and marvel at the amenities I enjoy, as well as my very active lifestyle and my productivity level (six books since coming to Woodland Pond, one play and four one-act plays—performed by our Playreaders group to an appreciative audience, plus my monthly article about Board doings for our newsletter and all the hours I spend on Board matters), they usually say that while they wish they didn't have the time-consuming, pressured burdens of home ownership, they're not quite ready to make a change.

To this kind of comment I immediately reply, "Nonsense!" Then I stress how a Continuing Care

Retirement Community like Woodland Pond is primarily designed for active, healthy seniors who, unencumbered with home ownership, want to continue to live independently while enjoying services and amenities comparable to a beautiful resort and feeling secure about healthcare resources in the future. Every day at Woodland Pond for me is like a holiday, free from stress, and I'm sorry that I didn't move here earlier.

In a book published in 2012, titled ***Extraordinary Centenarians in America:*** Their Secrets to Living a Long Vibrant Life, the author noted, "The people I talked to seek joy and find joy. They also were totally outside themselves and always thinking of others." It's easy to discover, as I did, that these qualities are exemplified in the Woodland Pond community on a daily basis. The caring nature of our residents reminds me of Winston Churchill's statement, "We make a living by what we get, but we make a life by what we give."

Whenever I leave Woodland Pond for any stay elsewhere, be it overnight, a weekend or a winter vacation, upon my entering the driveway at the entrance of Woodland Pond, I'm always thrilled to discover how emotionally connected I am to my community and how happy, even excited, I am to be returning **home**. I've heard other residents express similar feelings, and perhaps that's the best testimony to the enriched lifestyle, zestful atmosphere and long-term security that Woodland Pond offers.

At the conclusion of Voltaire's satirical look at the world in his acknowledged masterpiece ***Candide,*** the central character, after viewing so many destructive forces subjecting mankind to hardships and misery, determines that he cannot face the world's problems with any optimism and will find a measure of peace only within a personal world created around friends and loved ones and the pursuit of one's private interests.

Cultivating one's garden is how Voltaire described this practical approach to happy living. I often think of this powerful piece of literature— actually a philosophical treatise disguised as a comic novel—as I go about my daily life at

Woodland Pond. In this beautiful and stimulating setting, I eagerly look forward to each new, rewarding day, grateful that after a long life blending both happy and tragic events in a wide, turbulent spectrum of experience, I have reached a peaceful and safe haven where I can contribute to my community and flourish in my environment,, sharing laughter, learning, love and joyful living with my peers.

.

70332053R00113

Made in the USA
Middletown, DE
26 September 2019